BERLITZ®

HUNGARY

1989/1990 Edition

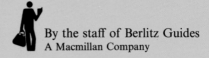

By the staff of Berlitz Guides
A Macmillan Company

How to use our guide

All the practical information, hints and tips that you will need before and during the trip start on page 160, arranged alphabetically with a list to enable easy finding.

For the general background see the sections Facts and Figures, p. 19, Introduction, p. 22, History p. 33.

If you are in a hurry and want to know the "musts", turn to the Essentials on p. 42.

All the sights to see are contained between pages 43 and 147. Our own choice of sights most highly recommended is pinpointed by the Berlitz traveller symbol.

All the activities and distractions you might want to know about (including eating out) are described between pp. 148 and 159.

The map section in the front of the book (pp. 6–18) will help you locate the sights you are looking for.

Finally, if there is anything that you cannot find, look in the complete index at the back of the book p. 188.

Photography: Eric Jaquier
Layout: Robert Rausis
© Cartography: Cartographia, Budapest

Acknowledgments
We wish to express our thanks to Vue Touristique I.P.V., Budapest and in particular to Professor Joseph J. Hollos for initiating and seeing this book through.

Copyright © 1983 by Berlitz Guides, a division of Macmillan S.A., Avenue d'Ouchy 61, 1000 Lausanne 6, Switzerland.

**4th Printing
1989/1990 Edition**

Library of Congress Catalog Card No. 82-84216.

Printed in Switzerland by Weber S.A., Bienne.

CONTENTS

CONTENTS

Although we make every effort to ensure the accuracy of all the information in this book, changes occur incessantly and rapidly. We cannot therefore take responsibility for facts, prices, addresses and circumstances in general that are constantly subject to alteration. Our guides are updated on a regular basis as we reprint. We are always grateful to readers, however, who let us know of errors, changes or serious omissions they come across.

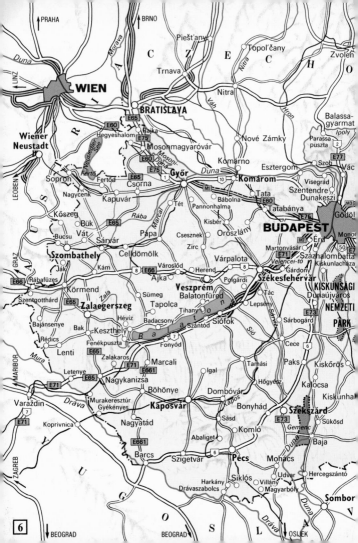

HUNGARY 7

SOPRON–GYOR REGION

BUDAPEST

NITRA
Nové Zámky
Komárno
Komárom
BUDAPEST
Mór
Várpalota
574
Váh
Čalovo
Ács
E75
Bábolna
Kisbér
Ácsteszér
Öreg Futóné
Tés
Kolárovo
E60
M1
10
Pannonhalma
Csesznek
Zirc
Körös-h.
704
Fenyőfő
Dunajská Streda
Vámosszabadi
Győr
Bakonybél
Duna
Mosoni-Duna
Abda
Tét
Rába
Moson-
magyaróvár
1
Pápa
BRATISLAVA
15
Csorna
Szany
Marcal
Celldömölk
E65
E75
Rajka
E60
E65
Rábca
Kapuvár
Répcelak
Rába
Sárvár
Fertőd
Fertőboz
Fertő-tó
Nagycenk
Répce
E65
Bük
Hegyfalu
Neusiedler See
Balf
Vát
Kőszeg
Szombathely
Eisenstadt
Fertőrákos
20 km
10 miles
Sopron
Károly-
magaslat
557
N
10
Bozsok
Bucsu
Velem
0
0

8

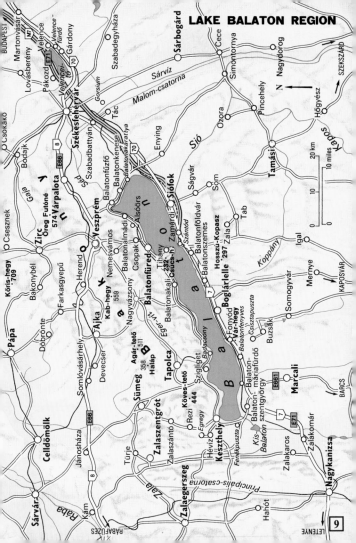

LAKE BALATON REGION

CENTRAL BUDAPEST
NORTH

SZENTENDRE

Perény út

Bécsi út

Vörösvári

Váradi S.

Gyenes

Kórház u.

Reménység

Sólymos

Szőlő

Solymár

Téglai

San

Bécsi út

FÖLD

ÓBUDA

Szentendrei

Kiscelli

Zápor

Kiscelli u.

Kiscelli-lejtő

Kenyeres

Selmeci u.

Kiscelli-parkerdő

Szomolnok

Bécsi

Mátyáshegyi út

Timár

Viador

Nagyszombat

Szőlő

Korvin Ottó

Timár u.

27 Táborvárosi Múzeum

Perc

Cserfés

26 Katonai Amfiteátrum

Kis-Kecske-hegy

Szépvölgyi

Alsó Zöldmáli

Felhévízi

Bécsi

Árpád fejedelem

Lajos

Duna

Premontrei templom 35

32 Szabadtéri Színpad

33 Domonkos kolostor romjai

31 Palatinus strand

Ferences templom romjai 34

Szemlő-hegy

Józsefhegyi

Cserje

Pálffy

Áfonya

Cinthalom

Vérhalom

Pálma

Árpád fejedelem

Hajós Alfréd

30 Hajós Alfréd uszoda

Mandula

Berkenye

Apostol

Felhalom

Borbolya

Frankel Leó

Komjádi Béla- 67 uszoda

25 Lukács gyógyfürdő

Áldás

Sólyom László

Bimbó

Bolyai

Gül Baba

Szemlőhegyi

Gül Baba türbéje 24

ROZSADOMB

Úttörőstadion 29

Centenáriumi emlékmű 28

Szent István park

Óbudai-sziget

Ákác köz

Laktanya u.

Miklós

Harrer Pál

Fő tér

Korvin O. tér u.

Hajógyár

Tavasz

Árpád

Duna

Magyar

0   300   600 m
0   300   600 yards

N

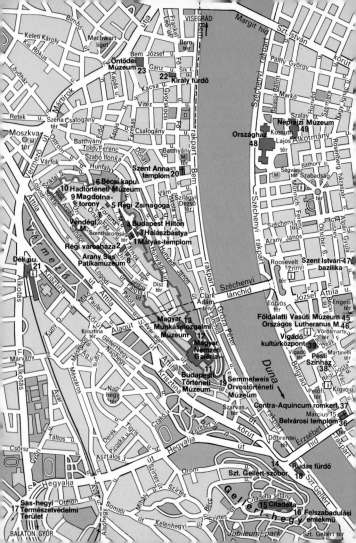

VÁCI út

Lenin krt

Váci út

Marx tér

Nyugati pályaudvar 55

Millenniumi emlékmű 60

Műcsarnok 62

Vajdahunyád vára 63

Hopp Ferenc Kelet-ázsiai Művészeti Múzeum 58

Ráth György Múzeum 59

Lövölde tér

Állami Operaház 57

Postamúzeum 56

Bélyegmúzeum 54

Keleti pályaudvar 51

Köztársaság tér

Zsidó Múzeum 52

Fővárosi Tanács 40

Főposta 44

Ferencesek temploma 41

Egyetem 42

Magyar Nemzeti Múzeum 50

Egyetemi templom 43

Iparművészeti Múzeum 53

CENTRAL BUDAPEST SOUTH

13

SZEGED

0   300   600 m

0   300   600 yards

BUDAPEST MAP KEY

1 Matthias Church
2 Former Town Hall
3 Fishermen's Bastion
4 Budapest Hilton Hotel
5 Former Synagogue
6 Vienna Gate
7 Museum of Commerce and Catering
8 Golden Eagle Pharmaceutical Museum
9 Church of St. Magdalene Tower
10 Museum of Military History
11 Budapest Museum of History
12 Hungarian National Gallery
13 Museum of the History of the Hungarian Working Class
14 St. Gellért Statue
15 Citadel
16 Liberation Monument
17 Eagle Hill Nature Reserve
18 Rudas Baths
19 Semmelweis Museum of the History of Medicine
20 St. Anne's Church
21 Southern Railway Station
22 Király Baths
23 Iron Foundry Museum
24 Gül Baba Tomb
25 Császár Baths
26 Military Amphitheatre
27 Roman Camp Museum
28 Centennial Monument
29 Pioneers' Stadium
30 National Sports Swimming Complex
31 Palatinus Swimming Complex
32 Open-Air Theatre
33 Dominican Convent Ruins
34 Franciscan Church Ruins
35 Premonstratensian Chapel
36 Inner City Parish Church
37 Contra-Aquincum Excavations
38 Pest Theatre
39 Vigadó Concert Hall
40 City Hall
41 Franciscan Church
42 University
43 University Church
44 Post Office
45 Underground Railway Museum
46 National Lutheran Museum
47 St. Stephen's Basilica
48 Parliament
49 Ethnographic Museum
50 Hungarian National Museum
51 Eastern Railway Station
52 Jewish Religious and Historical Collection
53 Museum of Applied Arts
54 Philatelic Museum
55 Western Railway Station
56 Postal Museum
57 State Opera House
58 Museum of East Asian Art
59 Museum of Chinese Art
60 Millenary Monument
61 Museum of Fine Arts
62 Art Gallery
63 Castle of Vajdahunyad
64 Zoo
65 Amusement Park
66 Széchenyi Baths

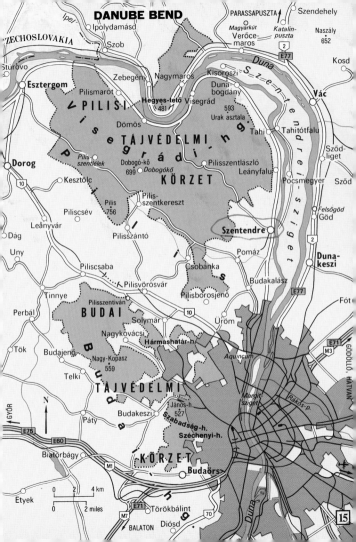

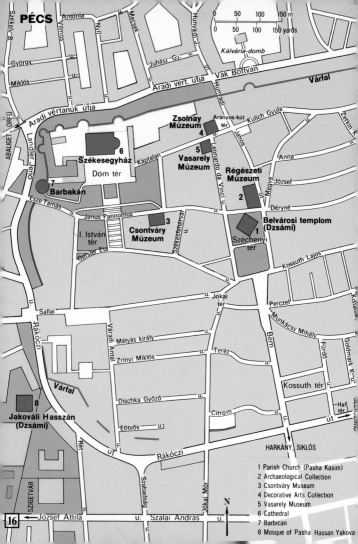

PÉCS

György

Miklós

Antónia

Vilmos

Mecsek

Nyíl

Juhász - Gy.

Vák Bottyán

Kálvária-domb

Aradi vért. útja

Hunyadi

Várfal

Aradi vértanúk útja

Zsolnay
Múzeum

4

Aranyos-kút
tér

Kulich Gyula

Zétkin S.

Landler Jenő u.

Dóm tér

6

Székesegyház

Káptalan

Vasarely
Múzeum

5

Leonardo da Vinci u.

Anna

Jahos

József

Régészeti
Múzeum

2

Magye

Déryné

Belvárosi templom
(Dzsámi)

1

Janus Pannonius u.

7

Barbakán

Esze Tamás

Csontváry
Múzeum

3

Széchenyi
tér

I. István
tér

Gsztszt Éta

Szkszfehérvár u.

Kossuth Lajos

Jókai
tér

Perczel

Sallai

Rákóczi

Váradi Antal

Mátyás király

Munkácsy Mihály

Bem

Kisfalu

Zrínyi Miklós

Teréz

Fürdő

Goldmárk K. u.

Várfal

Dischka Győző

Kossuth tér

8

Jakováli Hasszán
(Dzsámi)

Eötvös

Citrom

Hali
tér

út

Rét

Rákóczi

HARKÁNY, SIKLÓS

SZIGETVÁR

József Attila

Szabadság

Jókai Mór

Szalai András

N

1 Parish Church (Pasha Kasim)
2 Archaeological Collection
3 Csontváry Museum
4 Decorative Arts Collection
5 Vasarely Museum
6 Cathedral
7 Barbican
8 Mosque of Pasha Hassan Yakova

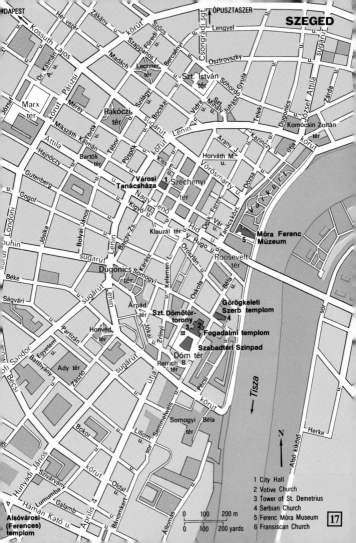

SZEGED

1 City Hall
2 Votive Church
3 Tower of St. Demetrius
4 Serbian Church
5 Ferenc Móra Museum
6 Fransiscan Church

17

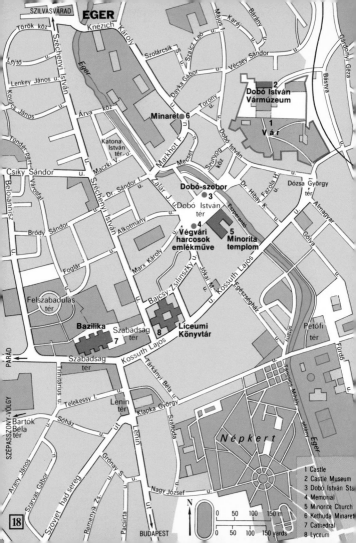

EGER

1 V á r
2 Dobó István Vármúzeum
Minarèt ● 6
Dobó-szobor ● 3
Dobó István tér
4 Végvári harcosok emlékműve
5 Minorita templom
Bazilika
7 Szabadság tér
8 Líceumi Könyvtár

Népkert

1 Castle
2 Castle Museum
3 Dobó István Sta
4 Memorial
5 Minorite Church
6 Kethuda Minaret
7 Cathedral
8 Lyceum

N

0   50   100   150 m
0   50   100   150 yards

18

BUDAPEST

FACTS AND FIGURES

Geography: Area 35,919 square miles, slightly larger than Austria, but half the size of Oklahoma or Missouri. Landlocked Hungary borders on Austria, Czechoslovakia, the Soviet Union, Rumania and Yugoslavia. Most of the terrain, a fertile plain, lies less than 655 feet above sea level. Low mountain ranges in the north reach 3,300 feet (Mount Kékes). Hungary's biggest river, the Danube (*Duna*), forms the border with Czechoslovakia in the north-west and then flows north to south through the country. 230-square-mile Lake Balaton is Central Europe's largest freshwater lake.

Population: 10,500,000 (in 1987), of which 50 per cent live in urban areas.
The density is 298 persons per square mile, and the population growth rate 0.4 per cent per year. Aside from the Hungarians, there are small minorities of Germans, Slovaks, Southern Slavs and Rumanians.

Major cities: Budapest (Pop. 2,090,000), Miskolc (210,000), Debrecen (200,000), Szeged (175,000), Pécs (170,000), Győr (125,000), Székesfehérvár (100,000)

Government: People's Republic led by the Hungarian Socialist Workers' Party. The National Assembly has executive powers, a Presidium fulfills the functions of head of state and the Council of Ministers carries out policies. Hungary is a founder-member of the Council for Mutual Economic Assistance (Comecon) and the Warsaw Pact.

Economy: Socialist with decentralized management, incentives for profitability and private operation of some consumer service outlets and supplementary production units. Principal exports: agricultural and food products, bauxite, buses, consumer goods, machinery, pharmaceuticals.

Religion: No official statistics are kept, but Catholics are clearly the strong majority.

Language: Hungarian. A widely understood second language is German, with English runner-up.

HUNGARY AND THE HUNGARIANS

Set right in the very centre of Europe, Hungary occupies the modest area of 35,919 square miles. But statistics miss the point. Although fifteen European countries are bigger, none can muster more hospitality, local co-lour or old-fashioned *joie de vivre*.

Occupying only one per cent of Europe's area, Hungary offers every kind of scenery except major mountains and seashore. By way of compensation for its land-locked predicament, nature has provided Hungary with middle Europe's biggest lake and a gener-ous share of one of the planet's most romantic rivers.

The Danube links two charm-

ing cities, Vienna and Budapest; in summer, fleet hydrofoils cut the trip to five hours or less. But whereas the river touches Vienna only peripherally—a sideshow—in Budapest the Danube is lifeline, main street and trademark. The great river cuts through the heart of the city, distancing the historic Buda hills from the elegant boulevards of Pest, yet enhancing the beauty of the whole.

With a population above two million—about ten times the size of any other town in Hungary—Budapest is the uncontested economic and cultural capital as well as the political powerhouse, where life is faster and more sophisticated than in the provinces.

But for all its allure to Hungarians and foreigners alike, Budapest has no monopoly on the country's historic, artistic

or recreational attractions. The smaller towns, too, are packed with monuments and museums, with Roman ruins and Gothic churches, Renaissance palaces and startling reminders of the years the Turks held sway over the Magyars.

And the countryside—where storks hold court atop telephone poles and shepherd dogs herd sheep for a living—has its own unspoiled charm. Hungary is so small that a few hours' drive takes you through landscape as varied as the weather—curvaceous hills, wheat fields and orchards, granite mountains, and pusztas that disappear into the horizon. The Hungarians were clever enough to declare the Hortobágy, the ancient part of the country's Great Plain (Nagyalföld), a national park. Elsewhere, wildlife sanctuaries, national parks and forests provide additional breathing space, ever more valuable in a country tilting toward the urban way of life. For the first time, the 1980 census, which counted 10,710,000 Hungarian noses, showed more than half the population living in the towns.

Anything can happen in Hungary when it comes to the weather. Halfway between the North Pole and the equator, the country is torn between the influences of the Atlantic, the Mediterranean, and the continental climate of eastern Europe and Asia. The annual mean temperature works out to a comfortable 10° C (50° F), but, again, statistics are shifty. The swings to hot and cold can be dramatic. The nicest part of the climate is the sunshine table. Southern Hungary catches an enviable 2,000 hours of sunshine in an average year, more than almost any of Europe's famous resort areas.

But in the event of rain, all is not lost for the tourist. Hungary counts about 450 museums; every little town shows off its archaeology or handicrafts, and the big towns have eminent museums of history and art. You can tour a castle or a cathedral, or you can go underground: the Aggtelek cave system is Europe's most extensive network of stalactite caves—a really impressive underground world. The rainy-day tourist can get into the swim at one of Hungary's 500 thermal baths. The medicinal waters are prescribed for any number of physical ailments, or just to unwind after a gruelling day. Apart from the steam, the baths have plenty of atmosphere, especially Budapest's authentic Turkish baths, which are architectural monuments from the 16th and 17th centuries.

Incidentally, Hungary is so bountifully supplied with hot

Fishermen's Bastion, reflected in Budapest Hilton Hotel façade.

25

springs that some urban areas are thus provided with central heating. And 30 per cent of the output of thermal wells goes to agriculture, heating 500,000 square metres of greenhouses.

Since prehistoric times a mystique has surrounded the hot springs of Budapest. The Romans, devout bathers, built elaborate establishments for the military force they assigned to the Danube hills. The site of modern Budapest was chosen as an important headquarters for the Roman empire's north-eastern frontier. A legion was assigned to keep the barbarians on the far side of the Danube. Inevitably, the foe crossed the river and crushed the defenders of western civilization. But Budapest rose again... and again and again.

Since the Dark Ages, due to the tragic recurrence of invasion, war and revolution, the city has had to be rebuilt with disheartening frequency. The excavated vestiges of imperial Rome maintain a low profile on today's skyline. There are a few monuments to be approached with awe, but also many restored buildings of advanced age, as well as admirable experiments of the 19th and 20th centuries. The most compelling slice of cityscape, in the Castle District of Buda, boasts a massive palace begun in the Middle Ages, the soaring barbed tower of an often-rebuilt 13th-century church, a

joyous Gothic folly less than a century old, and a glassy Hilton hotel built around the remains of an ancient monastery.

For all its familiar comforts, Budapest belongs, for a visitor from the West, to another world. The Ladas and Skodas jockeying for parking meters are just one reminder. But if your preconceptions about life in a People's Republic entail intrusive bureaucrats, ideological slogans, queues and surly waiters, you'll certainly find Budapest a surprise. Nobody will bother you; the slogans are just as likely to advertise TV sets or soft drinks; food and consumer goods are in plentiful supply; and when the waiter hands you the menu, he may actually click his heels!

But for visitors interested in politics and economics, Hungary offers a look at the workings of a different social system. There are big state-run factories and collective farms, but also an area of private initiative—family-operated. restaurants and shops, and a cornucopia of home-grown produce in the marketplace. The school-children wear red Pioneer kerchiefs, but they also don jeans and buy the latest western pop records. And, in a country where the role of religion in society has caused pain and controversy, you'll find the churches packed every Sunday.

The people of Budapest are

inordinately proud of their bridges, perhaps because of their relative novelty. The first permanent span didn't go into service until 1849; the Chain Bridge was a great engineering achievement, for it crosses the Danube at a point where the river is wide and swift and prone to break up into ice-floes in the spring. Also, the older generation remembers Budapest at the end of World War II, when German demolition squads had blown up all the bridges and people had to rely on ferries and pontoons. So the sight of a hydrofoil skimming beneath the arching bridges means a lot.

Many an admiring glance is dedicated to the chic women of Budapest. Not all of them can look as glamorous as those ageless Hungarian exports, the Gabor sisters, but that same vivacity and flair often shines through. The government, aware of the importance of this natural resource, makes sure the city is well supplied with modern hairdressing establishments. They open as early as 6 a.m. for the convenience of customers who need a pick-me-up on the way to the factory.

The Hungarians conform to no stereotype in physical appear-

*Naive painting
from the Hungarian
National Museum, Budapest.*

ance, though the men often possess assertive noses; droopy Pancho Villa moustaches work well here. Otherwise, there are high-cheekboned blondes and round-faced brunettes and swarthy men with thick black hair and blue-eyed red-heads to confuse the issue.

But, with middle age, most show the toll of all those strudel snacks, thickening around the middle in spite of the calisthenics classes so prominent on TV.

Visitors soon understand that in Hungary—as in France or China—good food plays an exceptionally important role in life. With all the gourmet restaurants and enticing pastry shops, this is a perfect place to abandon a diet.

Though Hungarian cooks are known abroad for their devotion to paprika, they are by no means narrow-minded about spices; the cuisine, quite varied, is first-class. Restaurants may be big and expensive or small and intimate, country inns or fishermen's bistros. In many of them, dinner is almost inevitably accompanied by the music of gypsy violins—and wine, candlelight and gushing music are not only for the tourists.

For livelier evenings, the big towns have nightclubs and discos. You may be surprised to discover nightlife tours as a standard feature of Budapest's tourist circuit. "The Paris of the East"

really does have nightspots with statuesque showgirls and cabarets, plus other late-night establishments with live music and dancing. The revelry continues around town until 5 in the morning. Budapest also has a couple of gambling casinos where roulette, baccarat, blackjack and one-armed bandits accept deutsche marks only—but only until 2 a.m.

On a more uplifting note, try the concert, opera and ballet scene. Theatres in all the towns, heavily subsidized by the government, put on busy seasons of classic and modern works with startlingly cheap ticket prices. The widest choice of attractions, predictably, is found in Budapest. What other city of its size supports two opera companies and four professional symphony orchestras? Not to mention chamber music, operetta and folk groups. In the land of Liszt and Bartók, music holds a special place of honour.

In summer much of the musical and theatrical life moves outdoors. Some of the settings are unforgettable: in Szeged, the neo-Romanesque Votive Church is the backdrop, with seats under the stars for an audience of more than 6,000. Elsewhere, castles, cathedrals, even caves are commandeered for summer festival events.

For many visitors, outdoors means sports. Horseback riding, for experts or beginners, is the central feature of a number of specialized Hungarian holidays. Dozens of riding schools and ranches in all regions are involved. Hungary has been a horse-breeding country to reckon with ever since the Magyars galloped in from the east a thousand years ago.

Foreign visitors also take advantage of packaged hunting holidays aimed at big or small game. And fishermen, swimmers and boating fans look to Hungary's lakes and rivers for their fun.

Sightseeing in Hungary is a nicely balanced mixture of natural delights, historic monuments and towns of character. For instance: a few miles upstream from Budapest the Danube changes course in a rambling horseshoe bend. The broad river sweeps so majestically between near and distant mountains that you'll wonder why the Danube evoked only a famous waltz... instead of a symphony or a hymn. The towns of the Danube Bend, as the area is called with more logic than poetry, are charming: Szentendre, with its brightly painted old houses exuding a whiff of the Mediterranean; the cathedral city of Esztergom; and, between them, the riverside palace of King Matthias at Visegrád.

Hungary's most popular recreational area surrounds Lake Balaton, the inland sea only an hour's drive south-west of Bu-

dapest. The nearby villages and vineyards add to the picturesque appeal.

Close to the western frontier, some of Hungary's most memorable tourist attractions are within easy reach of Austrian and German visitors. But whichever direction you come from, the winning medieval town of Sopron should not be missed. Kőszeg's Renaissance streets have been restored for a stroll. And beyond the old Roman capital of Szombathely, the obscure village of Ják is crowned by a perfect Romanesque church.

Southernmost Hungary—the region of the Transdanubian hills—is rich in scenery, history and culture. In the city of Pécs, founded by the Celts and developed by the Romans, the principal parish church first served as a Turkish mosque. (You can still find the prayer niche pointing toward Mecca.) Hungary's biggest wildlife preserve, the Gemenc national forest, is home for deer, wild boar and waterfowl—viewable from a narrow-gauge tourist railway or excursion boats.

Eastwards from the Danube, the Great Plain is more than just endless fields of grain: forests and rivers, swamps and spas, cattle ranches and bird sanctuaries. The main city of the southern plain, Szeged, has an efficient town plan, thanks to the devastation of

an 1879 flood. The Tisza river may not have the international reputation of the Danube but it does offer lovely pastoral scenery for excursions.

Between the Danube and the Tisza, the Kiskunság National Park is made up of six scattered enclaves, each with its own wild attractions. Coachloads of tourists roll in for the horse shows. The Hungarian version of cowboys may also be seen in action in the Hortobágy National Park, east of the Tisza. The puszta has inspired poets and artists, and many a tourist, with its haunting landscape.

Continuing counter-clockwise around the country, the Northern Highlands run to impenetrable forests and hills high enough to appeal to the local skiers. Two towns are "must" attractions in the north-east: Eger, with a historic castle and a thrilling skyline climaxed by a slender minaret preserved from the age of the Turkish occupation, produces Bull's Blood, the powerful dark-red Hungarian wine. Then there is Tokaj, a perfect picture postcard of a village, the home of the legendary Tokay wine.

One of the pleasant things about Hungary is the diversity of dependable wines, mostly quite inexpensive. From north to south

Folklore group, Bugac.

and west to east, you keep coming across vineyards and cellars, even in the kind of countryside not usually associated with wine. Only about one-third of Hungarian vines grow on hillsides; the rest fan out over the flatlands, businesslike but still enjoying all that sunshine. And while you're investigating the regional wines you can collect some local recipes: Szeged fisherman's soup, Hortobágy pork cutlets, Debrecen sirloin, Baja stuffed peppers.

For the average foreign tourist, Hungarian is, admittedly, a hopeless mystery. The key to getting along is German, even a smattering. For historical reasons (such as the old Austro-Hungarian empire), German is understood by almost everyone you'll meet in Hungary. For more recent historical reasons, Russian is studied by every schoolchild, though rarely spoken. English comes out third.

But even if you're reduced to gestures and grimaces, the Hungarians have time, patience and goodwill for the foreign tourist. You'll feel the old world hospitality everywhere you go, in Budapest or in a hamlet with an unpronounceable name. You can go anywhere you please in Hungary, at your own pace, with or without advance planning... a land for spontaneous discoveries and pleasures.

31

HISTORY

Any connection between the Huns and the Hungarians is purely coincidental. It's true that the most dreadful Hun, Attila, used to operate in the neighbourhood in the 5th century, but the real Hungarians didn't arrive on the scene until several centuries later. The similarity of names, which carries over into several languages, confused some medieval chroniclers. The early Hungarians rather liked being mistaken for Huns; it encouraged potential foes to keep their distance.

The first Hungarians conquered the land in the 9th century; the traditional date is 896. They were horsemen and warriors, but also farmers, hunters and fishermen, and they wandered a long way before they reached the Carpathian basin. Their home base is thought to have been between the river Volga and the Ural mountains. (Related tribes from the same homeland ended up in Finland. Specialists label both the Finnish and Hungarian peoples, and their strange, mutually incomprehensible languages, as Finno-Ugric.) The first great Hungarian leader, Prince Árpád, founded a dynasty which led Hungary into statehood. Árpád's tribe was known as the Magyars;

Houses of Parliament, Budapest.

33

Roman wall fresco, Óbuda.

later, all Hungarians were to call themselves Magyars, and the tribe's name became the name of the country and language also.

At the Beginning

As for the history of the land, the preamble goes back hundreds of thousands of years. Less than 40 miles west of Budapest, at the village of Vértesszőlős, human traces thought to be half a million years old have been excavated. The bones of these early men are displayed at the Hungarian National Museum.

The tribes that migrated to the area in prehistoric times brought new skills and tools which improved a hunter's odds, made farming feasible and permitted the rise of primitive industries. And tenuous trade routes were established which linked Hungary with more sophisticated societies thousands of miles away. At the start of the Iron Age, when the Scythians rode onto the scene, local workshops were producing weapons, pottery and jewellery.

In the 3rd century B.C. Hungary was occupied by Celtic warriors, retreating from defeat in Greece. They established a tribal centre atop Budapest's Gellért Hill, commanding the Danube. The Celts were responsible for major advances in many areas.

But the full benefits of western civilization didn't reach Hungary until the 1st century A.D. with the conquering legions of the Roman empire. The strategy of the Emperor Augustus (27 B.C.–A.D. 14) pushed the north-east frontier of the empire to the Danube. By the 2nd century perhaps 20,000 Roman soldiers were deployed along the river between Vienna and Budapest alone, manning the main line of defence against the barbarians.

To command and coordinate this long, exposed perimeter, the Romans built Aquincum, a military camp which soon spawned civilian suburbs laid out as straight as troops on parade. In A.D. 106, the outpost became the capital of the Roman province of Lower Pannonia. The importance of Aquincum can be judged by the magnitude and beauty of the Roman vestiges unearthed in widely separated areas of present-day Budapest.

Other towns west of the Danube also prospered under Roman rule. Savaria (today's Szombathely) became the capital of Upper Pannonia in A.D. 107; its most impressive ancient ruin, the Sanctuary of Isis, wasn't discovered until the 1950s. As you wander through Sopron—called Scarbantia in the Roman era—you could easily walk right past a Gothic cellar filled with a hoard of Roman statues, tombs and tablets. A few miles away, the extraordinary stone quarry of Fertőrákos was first exploited by the Romans, who built the original thermal baths at nearby Balf.

When the overstretched Roman empire began to give, tribes as fearsome as the Vandals and Huns moved in for the kill. The Dark Ages enveloped Hungary. Waves of nomads pushed, or were pushed, ever westwards across the land. For better or worse, the only period of relative stability came during the occupation by the Avars. But they, too, were driven out, by Charlemagne. Within a century the Magyars had arrived, armed with bows and arrows. The pastures and forests, rivers and lakes appealed to them, and they decided to stay.

The Hungarians

On Christmas Day in the memorable year of A.D. 1000, Hungary crowned its first king, Stephen I. Like his father, Prince Géza, King Stephen accepted Christianity and the authority of the pope; he was to attain sainthood.

A landmark of 1222, the Golden Bull—a sort of Magyar Magna Carta—spelled out the rights of the citizens, nobles and freemen alike. But civilization suffered a tragic setback in 1241, when the country was overrun by Mongol hordes.

King Béla IV set about reviving the young nation from the wreckage. He granted a new charter for the reawakening city of Pest and, across the Danube, founded the town of Buda on a plateau which he prudently enclosed within walls.

With the end of the Árpád dynasty in 1301, a series of foreign kings ruled Hungary—a cosmopolitan royal roster drawn from all over Europe. In the middle of the 15th century, a hero emerged to rally not only the Hungarians, but other Christian peoples as well. János Hunyadi, the viceroy of Hungary, led the armies which turned back a long-threatening and seemingly invincible Turkish juggernaut. His 1456 triumph at Nándorfehérvár (now Belgrade) is remembered to this day by Catholics all over the world; and in commemoration, church bells ring and the Hungarian radio even relays the toll of the angelus every noon.

The son of János Hunyadi, known as Matthias Corvinus, reigned as Hungary's king from 1458 to 1490, a golden age of civic and intellectual development. Buda became an advanced centre of Renaissance culture and Pest flourished in trade and industry. King Matthias employed Italian artists to expand and beautify the Royal Palace on Castle Hill.

16th-Century Defeats

With the death of Matthias, feuding noblemen squabbled over the succession, reversing the movement towards national progress and security. An army of peasants, led by György Dózsa, rose in rebellion in 1514, but the insurrection failed and the leaders were tortured to death; harsh laws were enacted to reinstate the ancient deprivations of the serfs.

All the while, the Turks had been massing for war against a weakened Hungary. The fateful battle was fought near Mohács, on the Danube, in 1526. The invaders killed Hungary's King Louis II and much of the army he led. In a slow-motion disaster, the Turks finally occupied Buda in 1541. The nation was demoralized and dismembered: the north and west fell to the Habsburg empire, Transylvania became a so-called independent principality under Turkish hegemony, and central Hungary bowed under direct Turkish rule.

Occupation by the Ottomans ushered in an era of inertia, rather than oppression. During the century and a half of Ottoman rule, little was accomplished apart from the construction of fortifications and public baths. Visitors were appalled to find Buda decaying, and an official who went to the other side of the river despaired: "Alas, poor Pest! Pestilence should be thy name." But the worst was yet to come. Pest and later Buda were subjected to long, devastating sieges before the

Turks were finally routed by the armies of allied Christian powers. In 1686 Buda, "liberated", lay in ruins.

Under the Habsburgs

With the dominion of the pashas at an end, Hungary found itself under the stern administration of the Habsburgs. Dissatisfaction festered, and in 1703 Hungarians went to war for independence. The leader was a Transylvanian prince with a handlebar moustache, Ferenc Rákóczi II. Outnumbered and betrayed, the Hungarians lost the struggle in 1711.

But the Vienna connection meant more than just political subjugation. The country took great economic strides in the 18th century as a Habsburg province. Factories, theatres and newspapers were opened; Pest expanded its role in international trade and Buda was restored to its position as Hungary's administrative centre.

In the middle of the 19th century, Hungarians fought a new war for independence from the Habsburgs. The initial rebellion of 1848 was led by the poet Sándor Petőfi, but he was cut down in battle at the age of 26. To crush the insurrection, Emperor Franz Josef I summoned help from the

Wooden statue of warrior, Mohács Memorial Park.

Tsar of Russia. The combined Austrian and Russian armies finally triumphed in August 1849. The revolutionary statesman Lajos Kossuth, who had headed a provisional government, and other leaders of the independence struggle fled the country.

Defeat was followed by political repression, but economic advancement gradually resumed. Soon after peace returned to Hungary, the Budapest Chain Bridge inaugurated uninterrupted year-round traffic across the Danube; a railway was opened between Pest and Vienna; and trading began on the Pest stock exchange. In 1873 the cities of Pest, Buda and Óbuda—with a combined population approaching 300,000—merged into the metropolis of Budapest, big and strong enough to be the nation's undisputed capital.

A new political framework had been created in 1867. Under a compromise designed to curtail home-rule agitation, the Austro-Hungarian empire was established. Hungary was granted its own government, but key ministries were shared with the Austrians. The Dual Monarchy, as it was called, set the stage for the 20th century's jolting political changes.

Into War and Revolution

Hungary fought World War I on the losing side. As part of the Austro-Hungarian empire, the country was obliged to aid its German allies. Hundreds of thousands of Hungarian troops died on two fronts, and at home the hardships multiplied.

In October 1918, the monarchy was toppled by what is now referred to as the Bourgeois Democratic Revolution. King Charles IV of Austria-Hungary, crowned Hungarian king in Buda's Matthias Church less than two years earlier, was deposed to make way for the Hungarian Republic.

This was soon displaced by a short-lived Hungarian Soviet Republic. Among the leaders were Hungarians who had participated in the Bolshevik revolution and army veterans who had become communists while prisoners of war in Russia. The proclamation of a Hungarian dictatorship of the proletariat was vigorously opposed in many circles. It was overthrown after only 133 days in power.

The new right-wing regime, headed by Admiral Miklós Horthy, initiated a purge. Meanwhile, reprisals of another sort were laid out in the Treaty of Trianon (1920), which punished Hungary for its role in World War I. About two-thirds of Hungary's territory was handed over to its neighbours. Shrunk in size and spirit, torn by strife and crippled by economic problems, Hungary heard a vengeful voice from across the border: Adolf Hitler was promising a new order.

Hungary slipped into World War II in a series of small, reluctant steps: German troops were allowed to cross Hungarian territory and a Hungarian force was sent to help Hitler fight the Soviet Union. But the Horthy government nimbly avoided total involvement on the Axis side until March 1944 when the Germans occupied Hungary. This precluded a separate peace.

As the Soviets moved closer to Budapest, a Hungarian fascist regime led by Ferenc Szálasi was installed to support the Germans in a fight to the death. The final siege went on for weeks. When the Red Army finally secured all of Budapest on February 13, 1945, the capital could count only one out of every four buildings intact.

People's Republic

Post-war Hungary was transformed from a republic (1946) into a People's Republic (1949). Radical new economic directions were spelled out in a Three-Year Plan, followed by Five-Year plans. The government and party were led by Mátyás Rákosi, who was dismissed in 1956 for what are described as serious political crimes, personality cult and economic mistakes. It was a year of tumultuous change for Hungary.

"The events of 1956", an uprising which resulted in a heavy toll of life and property, as well as the exodus of more than 200,000 Hungarians to the West, broke out in Budapest on October 23. Within days, an interim coalition was formed. Headed by Imre Nagy, it proclaimed Hungary's neutrality and withdrawal from the Warsaw Pact. On November 4, with Soviet troops in Budapest, a new communist-led government was announced, directed by János Kádár.

When it was all over, the new administration set about improving economic conditions and relaxing the earlier political severities. The new slogan, "He who is not against us is with us", reversed the previous hard-line dictum and meant that average Hungarians could go about their daily lives without harassment. The standard of living visibly improved. Millions moved into new housing. Hundreds of thousands were able to buy cars and take holidays in the West.

Every year, the number of foreigners visiting Hungary greatly exceeds the country's population. The border they cross is notable for a refreshing effort at de-emphasizing red tape. The scars of wars and revolutions have now all but disappeared. The monuments to past trials and glories, alongside the new accomplishments, are open to inspection.

Complications Unlimited

"Thank you" is written köszönöm. In Hungarian it's not enough to dot your i's; you have to put in all those umlauts, accents and even odder diacritical marks. Such fussy details help to explain why so many outsiders despair of mastering the challenging Magyar tongue.

Furthering the feeling of foreignness, only a handful of international words carry over into Hungarian. You may recognize garázs (garage), posta (post office), trolibusz (trolleybus) and a few more, but even such universal words as hotel, police and restaurant are different in Hungarian.

On the other hand, several Magyar words have enhanced other languages: czardas (from the music played at the wayside inn called a csárda); goulash and paprika; and coach—a four-wheeled carriage developed in the 15th century in the Hungarian village of Kocs (pronounced coach)!

Magyars to Remember

Because of the obscurity of their language, perhaps, Hungarian authors and·poets have won little fame abroad. Conversely, when it comes to universal abstractions, the country has produced more than its share of notables.

In science, several Hungarians won fame in the United States: Nobel laureate Albert Szent-Györgyi, atomic pioneers Leo Szilárd and Edward Teller, and cybernetician John von Neumann. Péter Goldmark cut his niche in history by inventing the LP record.

Hungarians have played second fiddle to nobody in the musical world since Franz Liszt opened his academy in his Budapest home. Twentieth-century composers, conductors and soloists from Hungary include Béla Bartók, Zoltán Kodály, Antal Doráti, Eugene Ormándy, Sir George Solti, George Széll and Joseph Szigeti.

Hungarian artists, too, have achieved international recognition: László Moholy-Nagy, famed for his constructions; Marcel Breuer, architect and designer associated with the Bauhaus; and Victor Vasarely, the op art painter.

One field in which Hungarians have excelled from the beginning is the cinema. Among legendary film-makers, Sir Alexander Korda was born Sándor Korda, and director Michael Curtiz began his career as Mihály Kertész. Some memorable actors with Hungarian roots are Leslie Howard, George Sanders and Béla Lugosi.

Hungarian folk carving, Kalocsa.

THE ESSENTIALS

All too often, travellers are pressed for time; they need to know what they should at all events not miss and what the "musts" and "desirables" are in any one place. We propose the following list, but point out that inevitably there is an arbitrary and subjective element in our choice. The suggestions below are merely intended to help decide between alternatives.

Budapest:
Castle District
Matthias Church
Fishermen's Bastion
Royal Palace
Buda
Rudas, Király Baths
Chain Bridge
Aquincum ruins
Pest
Inner City Parish Church
Parliament
National Museum
Museum of Applied Arts
Museum of Fine Arts

(3 days minimum)

Danube Bend:
Szentendre old town
Visegrád royal palace
Esztergom: town, royal palace and Christian Museum

(1 day)

Western Border Region:
Sopron walled town
Fertőd palace
Kőszeg walled town
Szombathely ruins
Ják church

(3 days)

Balaton Region:
The Lake
Tihany peninsula
Badacsony mountains
Sümeg fortress
(en route) Székesfehérvár

(3 days)

Southern Hungary:
Pécs Roman and Turkish aspects
Mohács memorial park
Kalocsa town and folklore

(2 days)

Great Plains:
Kiskunság National Park
or
Hortobágy National Park
Szeged
Gyula castle

(2–3 days)

Northern Highlands:
Eger: town, fortress and
Inner City
Bükk mountains
Aggtelek caves
Tokaj town and vineyards

(3 days)

WHERE TO GO

A reasonable starting point for any survey of Hungary is Budapest, where you can see the most complete cross-section of the country's history and culture, from extensive Roman ruins to Art Nouveau apartment blocks. And almost all the other aspects of the nation's heritage can be sampled in the capital's museums.

The sights of Budapest are scattered all over the city's 200 square miles, so you can't expect to accomplish much on foot. Fortunately, public transport is highly developed and cheap. Peppy yellow tram-cars supplement the bright-blue fleet of buses; and below ground, the metro system manages to be both hygienic and efficient. The taxi service—including hundreds of private cabs—is good, with moderate fares.

How to see the rest of Hungary depends on you. A car provides the most flexibility. The railways link all the principal towns. Bus service extends to every hamlet with more than 200 inhabitants. Tourist excursions by coach cover many of the highlights.

Beyond Budapest we have divided the country into six regions, which we approach in a circuit running more or less counter-clockwise from the capital. Each area has its own scenic high-spots and cultural peculiarities.

Our provincial survey starts in the Danube Bend, just north of Budapest, where the rushing river forms the frame for centuries of history. From there we head for the western border region, with its faithfully restored medieval towns and castles. Between this area and the Transdanubian hills, Lake Balaton is more than just a playground; it's a focus of history, wine-making and industry. In Southern Hungary, the hills and forests surround towns as distinctive as Pécs, a glory of Romanesque and Turkish architecture. Eastwards, on the Great Plain and Puszta, the folklore comes alive. Finally, we look at the Northern Highlands, where Hungary's low-profile mountain ranges offer recreational possibilities and a Baroque town as fetching as Eger.

Don't try to see it all unless you have a couple of months to spare. Give yourself time to take in the sights and landscapes calmly, and to appreciate the charm of the place. For Hungary is very much a country of mood and atmosphere and these can best be savoured and absorbed at a leisurely pace. Better see less but take in the special beauty, than more but at a gallop.

BUDAPEST

Buda and Pest look like pieces from two different jigsaw puzzles which fit quite by chance. Hilly Buda is the last frontier of the Transdanubian mountains; in Pest, across the river, begins the Great Plain, stretching east, as flat as Kansas.

The attractions are too varied and widely dispersed to absorb in a quick, easy survey. Though the various coach excursions serve as a useful introduction, the city is most easily approached by degrees—a bit of Buda and a part of Pest, then back across the river again.

For reasons of organization, though, we have split the city into halves along the course of the Danube. We begin in Buda, covering the Castle District, the hills

beyond, ancient Óbuda and other riverside precincts on the right bank. Then over to Pest with its boulevards, shops and museums. In between, we cast a glance at Margaret Island, a quiet green isle equidistant from the urban pressures of Buda and Pest.

The best place to start, most would agree, is in the Buda Castle District, with its concentration of history and art... and its views.

THE CASTLE DISTRICT

This fascinating zone of cobbled streets, hidden gardens and medieval courtyards hovers above the rest of Budapest on a long, narrow plateau. Dozens of historic and beautiful buildings are concentrated here. Every second

*Danube panorama with
St. Gellért statue.*

house, it seems, bears a plaque identifying it as a *műemlék* (monument). You can walk uphill from the river—or ride the vintage train *(sikló)* that shuttles between a terminus at Clark Adam tér and the Royal Palace.

The spire of **Mátyás-templom** (Matthias Church) towers gracefully over the old town. Here the 15th-century King Matthias wed Beatrice of Aragon. Founded by King Béla IV in the 13th century, the parish Church of Our Lady is also known as the coronation church. The Emperor Franz Josef I was crowned here as king of Hungary in 1867, to the tune of Liszt's *Coronation Mass,* composed for the occasion.

During the Turkish occupation, the church was converted into the city's main mosque. Today visiting Hungarians pause reverently at the **Loreto Chapel,** in the south-west corner of the church, to regard a red marble statue of the Virgin. According to legend, the Turks buried the statue inside one of the chapel walls, but the figure made a miraculous reappearance during the siege of 1686. The pasha's troops took this as a signal that their time was up and prepared to surrender Buda.

The church was rebuilt in Baroque style after the return of the Christian forces; in the 19th century it was totally reconstructed along neo-Gothic lines. This is the version which was reassembled during the long restoration programme that made good the destruction of World War II. The unusual abstract designs which decorate the interior and roof of the church date from the 19th-century refurbishing; the motifs are Hungarian, not Turkish.

The **church museum,** beginning in the crypt and rambling up and around, contains medieval stone carvings, sacred relics, historic vestments and works of religious art. Note that the Hungarian royal crown and coronation jewels on display are only replicas; you can see the genuine articles at the Hungarian National Museum in Pest.

In the centre of Szentháromság tér (Trinity Square), on which the church stands, a votive column crowded with statues of saints and angels recalls a bubonic plague epidemic of the 18th century. The survivors built the monument in gratitude for being spared.

The other buildings facing the square are very much a mixed bag. On the north side, a neo-Gothic structure put up at the beginning of the 20th century now serves as a residence hall for students. On the west side, a modern whitewashed brick building, a latter-day reflection of the surrounding architecture, houses a centre for visiting foreign journalists. Outside stands a contemporary statue of a long-haired man, nude but for his hat, holding a horn with which to broadcast the latest news. The Baroque two-storey white building with a jutting corner balcony is the former Town Hall. Below the balcony there's a statue of Pallas Athena, who carries a shield emblazoned with the coat of arms of the town of Buda.

A much grander monument rises on the far side of Matthias Church—an equestrian statue of King (and Saint) Stephen I, who made Hungary a Christian country. He wears both a crown and a halo.

Halászbástya (Fishermen's Bastion), on the eastern edge of Castle Hill, could pass as an authentic medieval monument in a remarkable state of repair. Actually, this Disneyesque array of turrets, terraces and arches was built at the beginning of the 20th century, just for fun. From here, the views over the Danube are glorious. The architect even provided arches at every turn, so photographers can hardly avoid artistic framing of their shots of the river, its bridges and the Pest skyline across the way.

Turning away from the Danube: the view westward from Fishermen's Bastion focuses on the startling and controversial six-storey reflective-glass façade of the **Budapest Hilton Hotel.** Hungarian architect Béla Pintér took the bold approach in his design for a modern hotel wedged between historic monuments. The hotel's main façade, facing Hess András tér, integrates the remains of a 17th-century Jesuit college formerly on the site. Parts of an adjoining 13th-century abbey have also been incorporated into the building. An ancient milestone uncovered during the excavation of the site is displayed in the lobby; it marked the boundary of the Roman empire.

Hess András tér is named after the man who ran Buda's first printing shop, right here, in the 1470s. (Like the Chinese, the Hungarians put the last name first; we would call the printer András Hess.) The statue in the little square honours Pope Innocent XI for his help in organizing the army which finally routed the Turks from Buda. Notice the amusing bas-relief of a hedgehog on the house at No. 3; in the 18th century, it was an inn called the Red Hedgehog.

Historic Streets

The quaint Castle District lends itself to relaxed roaming with no hard and fast itinerary. Only four streets wide at its most expansive, the plateau is a car-free zone easily covered on foot. Here are some of the highlights to look for, starting with the easternmost street.

Táncsics Mihály utca. No. 7: Beethoven lived for a while (in

1800) in this solid old building. Next door, at No. 9, an 18th-century ammunition dump became a 19th-century prison which held, among others, the statesman Lajos Kossuth and the writer Mihály Táncsics, after whom the street is now named. No. 16: note the 18th-century religious mural between the bow windows upstairs. No. 26: just inside the doorway ancient Jewish tombstones are displayed. This house served as a synagogue (*Régi Zsinagóga*) from the end of the 14th century and now contains an exhibition of architectural and artistic remains.

At the northern end of the street, **Bécsi kapu** (Vienna Gate) provides a reminder of the walled city of yore, although the actual gate is a reconstruction. A couple of appealing, intricately decorated 18th-century houses add to the charm of the square. Thomas Mann lived at No. 7 from 1935 to 1936.

Fortuna utca. The house at No. 4, a hotel in the 18th and 19th centuries, has been given over to the **Hungarian Museum of Commerce and Catering** (*Magyar Kereskedelmi és Vendéglátóipari Múzeum*). The furnishings of historic hotel rooms, restaurants and coffee houses are assembled here, along with original menus, table settings and waiters' liveries.

Fishermen's Bastion.

Tárnok utca. This southerly extension of Fortuna utca contains a number of fine Baroque buildings. At No. 14, now an "espresso" restaurant, the upper storey juts out, as it did in the Middle Ages. The geometric frescoes on the front walls date from the 16th century. Up the street, at No. 18, an 18th-century chemist's shop called the **Golden Eagle** (*Arany Sas*) now serves as a museum. The exhibits cover the development of pharmaceutical science from ancient times, both in Hungary and around the world. Some of the architectural elements of the shop itself, begun in the 15th century, are also of interest.

Országház utca, which means Houses of Parliament Street, is not, as you might think, on the wrong side of the river. Parliamentary sessions took place in the building at No. 28 at the turn of the 19th century. It now belongs to the Academy of Sciences. At No. 2 Országház utca, a restaurant occupies what was once a grand 15th-century mansion; the courtyard, reminiscent of a medieval cloister, is noteworthy. Several other buildings on this street incorporate picturesque medieval features, sometimes just beyond the doorway; don't be shy about peering into courtyards, just in case.

Úri utca. This street is a treasure-trove of medieval vestiges. In the entryways of Nos. 31,

32, 35, 36, 38 and 40, among other houses, you'll find groups of sediles—built-in seats. The 14th-century dwelling at No. 31 retains the original stone window frames. Whatever their ages, virtually all of the buildings in the area maintain the same roof-line, but differing colour schemes and embellishments make each one distinctive.

At the top end of Úri utca stands a rather bleak but venerable tower *(Magdolna-torony)*, all that remains of the Church of St. Mary Magdalene. There has been a church on this spot since the 13th century. During the Turkish occupation, it was the only one left in Christian hands; the Catholics and Protestants shared the premises. The church suffered particularly grave damage in the last days of World War II, when the German army high command was holding out in the district. Miraculously, the Gothic tower escaped destruction.

Tóth Árpád sétány. This promenade along the western ramparts of the Castle District offers panoramas of the Buda Hills, rather than any outstanding monuments. And in the valley below you can see some metropolitan aspects of Buda, including the white immensity of Southern Railway Station *(Déli pályaudvar)* and the cylindrical glass tower of the Budapest Hotel.

The northern end of the walk

is cluttered with cannon—historic cast-iron guns laid out on display. The building at No. 40, much bigger than it looks, houses the **Museum of Military History** *(Hadtörténeti Múzeum)*. The exhibits range from pikes, swords and crossbows to a self-propelled missile launcher and a Mig-21 (parked in the courtyard). Selected documents and relics illustrate Hungary's efforts at self-defence over the centuries.

The Royal Palace

Returned to its former splendour, the Royal Palace *(Budavári Palota)* monopolizes the southern skyline of the plateau. Construction began rather modestly under Béla IV in the 13th century, but succeeding monarchs were intent on impressing their countrymen.

Under the Ottoman empire the palace fell into disrepair and the remains were destroyed in the siege of 1686. During the 18th and 19th centuries reconstruction, renovation and expansion turned the building into approximately the neo-Baroque monument of today. But it had to be rebuilt from the ground up after the siege of 1945, when the palace served as command post for the German occupation forces. Earlier it had been the headquarters and residence of the reviled Admiral Horthy.

To reach the palace, its fortifi-

The Castle District (Bécsi kapu tér).

cations and museums, you can either descend on foot from Dísz tér, in the southern part of the Castle District, or take a long walk up through the nicely landscaped grounds from Szarvas tér, near the complex road system on the west side of Elizabeth Bridge. A special bus (marked "V") shuttles between the museums and Clark Adam tér, at the Buda end of the Chain Bridge. If you walk along the Szarvas tér route, notice the "turbaned" Turkish gravestones on the hillside.

The solid stone walls of the restored fortifications guarding the southern approaches to the palace are now curtained with ivy. You can climb the spiral stairs to the ramparts for delightful Danube views. Within the palace complex are three museums.

The **Budapest Museum of History** (*Budapesti Történeti Múzeum*) occupies the Baroque south wing. This exhibition throws light on 2,000 years of the city's history. Displays include Roman statues, early Magyar saddles and weapons, Turkish utensils and 19th- and 20th-century Hungarian documents and photographs. During the most recent reconstruction programme, forgotten floors of the palace were discovered beneath the parts known before the war.

The restored medieval passageways, fortifications and gardens now form part of the museum. Important sculptures from the 14th and 15th centuries also were uncovered, and they are on view in the Gothic Knights' Hall and the Royal Chapel. The sound of Gregorian chants coming from loudspeakers hidden in the chapel underlines the medieval aura.

The **Hungarian National Gallery** *(Magyar Nemzeti Galéria)* is installed in the central area of the palace, under the dome; the entrance faces the Danube. Within the bare historic walls, an impressive modern museum was created. Hungarian painters and sculptors from the Middle Ages onwards are represented. The artist best known abroad is the 19th-century painter Mihály Munkácsy, celebrated for his vast output of family scenes, portraits, landscapes and melancholy historical compositions. Note, too, the Impressionist Pál Szinyei Merse.

In the north wing, the **Museum of the History of the Hungarian Working Class** *(Magyar Munkásmozgalmi Múzeum)* proves popular with comradely delegations from abroad. Exhibits deal with exploitation under capitalism, the struggles of early Hungarian communists and recent triumphs. Ideology aside, art lovers will not want to miss the big collection of posters.

VANTAGE POINTS

Gellért-hegy (Gellért Hill) rises only 770 feet above sea level, but it looms right alongside the Danube, providing a perfect vantage point. The **panorama** of Pest and Buda, the bridges and river traffic suggest the short answer to the mystery of Budapest's universal appeal: the city is simply beautiful.

The hill and the district are named after the Italian missionary, St. Gerard (in Hungarian, Gellért), who converted the Hungarians to Christianity. His success was mostly posthumous, for his efforts were cut short when militant heathens threw him off the hillside into the Danube. A statue of the saint stands on the eastern slope at the approximate spot from which his martyrdom was launched.

At the summit of Gellért Hill sprawls a fortress with a deceptively ancient look about it. The **Citadella** (Citadel) was built in the middle of the last century. In the final struggle of World War II, the occupying German army held out here. In recent years, the renovation of the citadel has been earnestly pursued. The once-menacing walls, nearly 10 feet thick, now encircle a restaurant, café and hotel.

The conspicuous modern addition to the hilltop, a gargantuan Liberation Monument, can be seen from many parts of the city.

It is dedicated "To the heroic Soviet liberators from the grateful Hungarian people" for ousting the German occupiers. On the reverse side of the monument are engraved the names of Red Army soldiers who died in the struggle.

On the slopes below the Citadel lies a modern park, Jubileumi-park, dedicated on the 20th anniversary of the liberation. It is a focus for patriotic occasions, as well as everyday recreation.

Sas-hegyi Természetvédelmi Terület (Eagle Hill Nature Reserve), surrounded on all sides by the city, is described as a living outdoor museum. Nature lovers can try to identify the rare species of flowers, butterflies, birds… even snakes amid unusual rock formations. This hilltop sanctuary opens week-ends only; the rest of the time the flora and fauna have Sas-hegy all to themselves.

A cog railway *(fogaskerekű-vasút)* chugs to **Szabadság-hegy** (Liberty Hill) from a terminal across the road from the Hotel Budapest. Comfortable modern trains built in Austria ascend through suburban greenery, past admirable villas and gardens, into open spaces—ski country in season.

Near the last stop of the cog railway, the **Pioneer Railway** *(Út-törővasút)*, run by youngsters, begins its 7½-mile route. The narrow-gauge line traverses what would seem to be unexplored forest—but for the well-marked hiking trails all along the way. School-children in smart uniforms work as station-masters, switchmen, ticket-sellers and conductors; only the engine-drivers are adults.

Summer sightseers take over the ski-lift *(libegő)* for a "flight" of about a mile. The lower terminus is at 93 Zugligeti út, and the trip ends near the top of János-hegy (János Hill), altitude 1,735 feet. A look-out tower on the hilltop surveys a radius of more than 45 miles—but misty skies often blur that far horizon.

North of János-hegy and nearly as high (1,630 feet), Hár-mashatár-hegy offers another good look-out point for views of Budapest and the Danube. No funicular or other exotic means of transport goes to the top, but some interesting vehicles leave the hill in the opposite direction. The wind currents here make Hár-mashatár Hill an effective starting point for hang-gliders.

RIVERSIDE BUDA

After the aerial perspectives, the view from the river bank becomes more meaningful. People on the Pest quays never tire of gazing across the Danube to the skyline of Citadel and castle. Less obviously, from the Buda side the view of sophisticated though dead-level Pest has its share of curiosi-

53

ties and delights. And from either side, the bridges themselves, always in sight, add to the allure, stitching together the disparate halves of Budapest.

The area of prime interest to tourists extends north from Szabadság híd (Liberty Bridge), opened in 1896 as the Franz Josef Bridge. On the Buda side, the bridgehead is Szent Gellért tér (St. Gellért Square). The ponderous old Gellért Hotel, inaugurated in 1918, was badly damaged in the war but dutifully restored to its original Eclectic design. By no accident, the hotel was built alongside ancient hot springs and it remains a leading centre of medicinal baths. The swimming pool makes artificial waves.

View from the Citadel.
Left: Pioneer Railway.

The steep hillside comes right down to the river road as it runs north from the Gellért, finally retreating at the approaches to Elizabeth Bridge. This leaves room for another thermal bath between hill and river. **Rudas fürdő** (Rudas Baths) has been in business for 400 years. Though the building has been destroyed, rebuilt, enlarged and much tampered with over the centuries, a graceful Turkish dome still rises over one octagonal pool, creating a wonder of geometric contrasts as sunlight filters through openings in the cupola. The radioactive water here is also said to make a therapeutic drink.

Of all Budapest's bridges, the lightest on its feet is Erzsébet híd (Elizabeth Bridge), a 1960s successor to a turn-of-the-century span demolished at the end of the

55

last war. It's a suspension bridge in the manner of the Golden Gate of San Francisco. Crossing this bridge towards Buda, the head-on view takes in the St. Gellért monument high on the hillside, above a garden and man-made waterfall. The Buda-bound traffic disgorges onto a complicated system of viaducts and under-passes. In the parkland inter-spersed among all these engineer-ing projects you may notice another Turkish bath, Rácz fürdő, across the road from the north edge of Gellért Hill. A dome from the Turkish era still covers one bathing pool.

This is the old Tabán district of Buda, where the ferrymen and other noted characters used to live. Only a few houses are left. One of them, a restored Louis XVI mansion at 1–3 Apród utca, was the birthplace of Professor Ignác Semmelweis (1818–65). He discovered the cause of puerperal fever, greatly improving world life-expectancy tables. The upper floor of the building now shelters the **Semmelweis Museum of the History of Medicine** *(Semmelweis Orvostörténeti Múzeum)*. Multi-lingual guides in white smocks point out gruesome ancient surgi-cal instruments and anatomical models, and there are enlighten-ing exhibits illustrating the path of medicine from witch doctors' amulets to modern times.

Northward from the museum,

the riverside area has a character of its own. The hillside facing the Danube, leading up to the Royal Palace, is adorned with arcades, terraces, ceremonial staircases and neo-Classical statues. The ar-chitect of this scheme, Miklós Ybl (1814–91), who also designed the Basilica, the Opera House and other monumental buildings, is himself the subject of a monu-ment near the river.

The often-clogged traffic round-about at the Buda end of the Chain Bridge occupies Clark Adam tér, a square named, in back-to-front Hungarian style, in memory of a Scottish engineer called Adam Clark. He oversaw construction of the bridge, a won-der of 19th-century technology. The man who designed it, Wil-liam Tierney Clark, an English engineer, was no kin to Adam Clark. The **Széchenyi lánchíd** (Chain Bridge), the first across the Danube, was opened to traffic in 1849, blown up by German sappers towards the end of the last war, but soon rebuilt.

Straight ahead of the bridge, Adam Clark constructed a tunnel beneath the Castle District pla-teau. Left of the tunnel is the terminus of the vintage train that runs uphill to the Castle District. Because of the juxtaposition of bridge and tunnel, a standard Budapest joke claims the bridge is pulled into the tunnel when it rains, so the chains don't rust.

The street north from Clark Adam tér, Fő utca (meaning Main Street), follows the original Roman route linking the Danube military outposts. About half a mile north of the Chain Bridge, at **Batthyányi tér,** the metro, bus and tram systems meet the suburban railway; there's a boat station at this important junction, too. This is the best place in town for an all-encompassing view of the Hungarian Houses of Parliament, directly across the river. It has the effect of London's parliament building, with the Danube substituted for the Thames.

The terminal of the Vienna stagecoach used to be right around the corner and, on the west side of Batthyányi tér, an 18th-century hostelry was famous. The emperor and many dignitaries stayed at the White Cross Inn, a venue for carnival balls and festivities of the district, called Víziváros (Watertown). The palatial two-storey **Rococo building** has been preserved, but its role has changed a bit; now it's a nightclub.

Szent Anna templom (St. Anne's Church), on the south side of the square, reveals Italian influences on Hungarian architecture of the mid-18th century. Tall twin towers top the Baroque façade, which is embellished with statues. The oval-domed interior contains more 18th-century statues and frescoes.

Farther north along Fő utca, a crescent surmounts the dome of a Turkish bath established in the 16th century. **Király fürdő** (Király Baths), a rambling green stone building, expanded over the centuries as Baroque and neo-Classical additions were made. The authentic Turkish section has survived, with an octagonal bathing pool under the largest of the domes.

An offbeat attraction of this district, at 20 Bem József utca, is a 19th-century iron foundry, now operated as a museum *(Öntödei Múzeum)*. A statue honours the originator of the enterprise, a Swiss industrialist named Abraham Ganz. The factory maintained production from 1845 all the way to 1964 and was noted for its tramwheels. Museum exhibits follow the evolution of technology from the Iron Age to the 20th century and include some handsome examples of the founder's art—iron stoves, statues, ships' propellers and bells.

The main street of this area, Mártírok útja, curves gradually towards the Danube and finally leads its tram, bus and car traffic across Margit híd (Margaret Bridge). This connects with the southern tip of Margaret Island, then deflects from the conventional arrow-straight trajectory. Thus from certain angles the bridge appears to end in mid-air. But it really does reach Pest. The

57

big white post-war building at the bridgehead, in an architectural style reminiscent of government offices in Washington, D.C., is the Socialist Workers' Party headquarters. In Budapest slang the building is called the White House.

Back in Buda, hilly streets zigzag north-westward from the bridge approaches up to the **Gül Baba türbéje** (tomb). This meticulously preserved relic of the Turkish era stands at 14 Mecset utca. The mausoleum was built in the middle of the 16th century by order of the pasha of Buda. It covered the grave of Gül Baba, a well-known dervish whose funeral the sultan himself attended. After the expulsion of the Turks, the octagonal building was used for a time as a Jesuit chapel. Restoration in recent years has been enhanced by a gift of art works from the Turkish government.

Another reminder of the Ottoman occupation may be found farther north along the embankment, at the **Császár uszoda.** A rheumatological hospital has grown around the original Turkish bath, built about 1570 as Veli Bey's Bath. A hemispherical cupola covers an octagonal bathing pool, surrounded by four rectangular chambers. The water is rich in calcium and sulphur.

Eastern Railway Station.

ÓBUDA

Heavy traffic rumbles along Korvin Ottó utca, the principal artery leading out of Budapest to the north. At its intersection with Nagyszombat utca, the road travels alongside the almost flattened but instantly identifiable remains of a Roman amphitheatre, one of the biggest outside Italy. This is part of Aquincum, capital of the Roman province of Lower Pannonia, later called Óbuda (Old Buda).

The **Military Amphitheatre** *(Katonai Amfiteátrum)* as it is known to distinguish it from a smaller one a couple of miles to the north, dates from the 2nd century. Here, gladiators performed for the amusement of the Roman legionaries who guarded this far frontier. Up to 16,000 spectators could be packed in when the contest drew a full house. The events took place on an elliptical arena more than 140 yards long. After the fall of the empire, a fortress was built on the site, and in later centuries houses took over the floor of the all-but-forgotten stadium. The ruins were excavated and very partially restored starting in the 1930s.

At 63 Korvin Ottó utca, workmen building an apartment block came upon the remains of public buildings from the Roman era. They constructed the new house around the "digs" which now form part of the basement. The prize discovery was a hunting mural of an archer on horseback, a work of considerable grace. Details of the comprehensive heating and plumbing system can also be seen, and some artefacts found on the spot are displayed in this historic hideaway, known as the **Roman Camp Museum** *(Római Tábor Múzeum)*.

Elsewhere in Óbuda, the ruins of a large bathing installation built for the Roman legion have been uncovered and protected in what is now the basement of a house at 3 Flórián tér. (The museum entrance is around the corner in Kórház utca.) The complexities of the baths, central heating system and all, intrigue visitors. Archaeologists of the distant future may be fascinated by the area on the north-west side of Flórián tér, the site of Budapest's first major shopping centre.

The remains of a grand Roman residence known as **Hercules Villa** lie in and around a modern school at 21 Meggyfa utca. The villa contained the finest mosaic floors found in all Pannonia. The central panel of the most famous scene, said to portray Hercules and his wife Deianira, was created out of small squares of marble and basalt in the early 3rd century.

The most extensive of the Roman achievements to come to light in Budapest, the civil town of **Aquincum,** accommodated the artisans, merchants, priests and other non military personnel attached to the legion. All the elements of a civilized town are here, from running water to central heating. The foundations of villas, workshops and markets have been uncovered. Clumps of poplars enliven the expanse of walls, knee-high to chest-high, and a few columns have been reconstructed to help the imagination. More has yet to be unearthed.

The site extends just east of Szentendrei út, the highway which, as route 11, continues on to the town of Szentendre. If you're travelling on the suburban railway *(HÉV)*, get off at the Aquincum stop and cross the highway, then go under the railway bridge. An ordinary tram ticket suffices.

At the entrance to the excavations, you can buy an inexpensive leaflet including a map of the civil town pointing out such sights as the Sanctuary of the goddess Fortuna Augusta and the baths with their cold-, tepid- and hot-water pools.

An imitation Roman building on the site houses a **museum** of the statues, pots, glassware, coins, tools and objects of everyday Roman life found in the ground here. Surrounding the museum on three sides, the **lapidarium** overflows with sarcophagi, columns and stone-carvings. The original inscriptions, of course, are all in Latin, posing yet another linguistic challenge to the foreign visitor.

MARGARET ISLAND

The Roman empire's élite escaped the cares of the day on this island halfway between Aquincum and Pest. In later eras, princes and plutocrats took refuge in the peace and quiet of mid-Danube. Margaret Island *(Margitsziget)* still serves as a sanctuary, but for more than a century the ordinary citizens of Budapest have been allowed to enjoy it. Within sight of the busiest parts of town, the feather-shaped, forested island is insulated from all the noise and bustle. You couldn't dream of a happier prospect.

Margaret Island is 1½ miles long and a few hundred yards wide at the middle. With its ageless woods, vivid flowerbeds and varied recreational facilities, it's a favourite spot for sports, amusements or just meditating. The island has been kept virtually free of motor traffic. Except for summer Sundays, the birds often have the place to themselves.

The southern end of the island is joined to "mainland" Buda and Pest by Margaret Bridge, a modern replacement for the original 19th-century span. It was destroyed in 1944, with needless loss of life, when German demolition charges went off prematurely.

Near the southern tip of the island, a tall bronze monument—shaped like a Hungarian version of yin and yang—commemorates the centenary of the unification of Buda and Pest. Margaret Island, equidistant between the two, is the obvious place for it.

The sports establishments on the island include Pioneers' Stadium *(Úttörőstadion)*, the National Sports Swimming Complex *(Hajós Alfréd-uszoda)* and the huge Palatinus Outdoor Public Swimming Complex *(Palatinus strand)*. The Palatinus installation, with cold- and warm-water pools, can hold 20,000 swimmers and sunbathers. There's even an artificial wavemaker.

Alongside the turn-of-the-century water tower, an open-air theatre *(Szabadtéri Színpad)* presents concerts, opera and ballet performances in the summer. The theatre's immense stage is conducive to lavish sets and productions. The park has a separate open-air cinema.

Near the outdoor theatre, you can wander through the ruins of a **Dominican Convent** *(Domonkos kolostor romjai)* founded by the 13th-century Hungarian King Béla IV. He enrolled his daughter in the convent when she was 11 years old, and she never left. Her burial place is marked by a marble plaque. She was called Princess (later Saint) Margaret; the island is named after her.

Another archaeological site on the island reveals the remains of a 13th-century Franciscan church *(Ferences templom romjai)* and monastery. And then there is the **Premonstratensian Chapel** *(Premontrei templom)*, a 20th-century reconstruction of a 12th-century church. The bell in the tower is said to be the oldest in Hungary; it survived the Turkish demolition of the church because it was buried nearby.

The woods near the chapel are thickly populated with statues and busts of Hungary's foremost writers and artists.

In 1866 deep drilling operations on Margaret Island hit a gusher—scalding hot mineral water. Soon the island became well-known as a therapeutic spa for sufferers from a wide range of ailments, from rheumatism to nervous disorders. Two large, elegant spa hotels occupy the north end of the island.

PEST

The bulk of modern Budapest lies to the east of the Danube in what, until little more than a century ago, was the autonomous city of Pest. The government buildings, big stores, museums and nightlife are concentrated in Pest. There are no hills to climb on this side of the river, but plenty of worthwhile sights to see along bustling streets and imposing boulevards.

From the viewpoint of a Roman general defending Buda and western civilization, the Pest side of the river meant nothing but trouble. He could only stare out at the flatlands—badlands—and wonder when the barbarians would try to ford the Danube. In A.D. 294, to make it harder for any invaders to launch an amphibious attack, the Romans established an outpost on the left bank. They called it Contra-Aquincum, and it forms the very core of innermost Pest.

The medieval town grew around the Roman beachhead, evolving into a long, narrow strip, with the Danube to the west and defensive walls along the other sides.

The oldest church—indeed, the oldest surviving structure—in all of Pest is **Belvárosi templom** (Inner City Parish Church). It's hemmed in alongside the elevated approach road to Elizabeth Bridge. Viewed from the front it appears to be contemporary with several other nearby churches. The twin Baroque towers and the façade, with nicely balanced windows, date from the early 18th century and were restored twice thereafter. But the church was founded in the 12th century. Parts of the original Romanesque construction can be discerned, but these elements blend into the Gothic with little more than a ripple in the walls and roof. The Turks who occupied Budapest

Margaret Island.

in the 16th century turned the church into a mosque and carved a *mihrab* (prayer niche) on the chancel wall.

The plaza alongside the church, Március 15. tér, takes its name from the day in March 1848 when the revolution for Hungarian independence broke out in Pest. A sunken park created around the excavations of **Contra-Aquincum** catches the spring sunshine and excludes winter winds. Here children play amid the much-restored rockpile representing the 3rd-century Roman outpost. Above stands a modern fountain with statues symbolizing Roman legionaries in action.

An ornate two-storey structure, termed the only surviving Baroque mansion in Pest, lies just up the street in Pesti Barnabás utca. Notice the marker next to the doorway—a sculpted finger pointing to the level the Danube attained during the flood of 1838. A restaurant has operated in this building for 150 years.

Cobbled centrepiece of an expansive pedestrian zone, **Váci utca** is the Bond Street of Budapest. The narrow street tempts shoppers with the last word in Hungarian fashions, as well as art works and handicrafts. Several large bookstores along Váci utca

Shopping street (Kígyó utca) with Franciscan church.

sell Hungarian-published books in foreign languages. Here, too are the high-rise premises of the International Trade Centre and Central European International Bank, as well as the Taverna Hotel and entertainment complex.

Lift your eyes above shopwindow level and study some of the turn-of-the-century buildings on this street. They include intriguing experiments in modern architecture, notable for their unusual sculptural additions. An illuminated sign reading Pesti Színház (Pest Theatre) hangs over the street. In the entrance of the theatre a plaque observes that Franz Liszt made his Pest debut as a pianist here at the age of 12.

Váci utca runs into the busy yet relaxed square named after Mihály Vörösmarty, a nationalist poet and dramatist of the 19th century. Not many pastry shops become national monuments, but the establishment on the north side of the square, the Gerbeaud, certainly qualifies. It used to be owned by the Gerbeaud family of Swiss confectioners; enthusiasts say the quality of the cakes hasn't deviated since the old days. The sumptuous interior has been preserved, and in pleasant weather the terrace is popular with people-watching calorie-collectors.

A concert hall has stood on the site of the newly refurbished **Vigadó** since 1832, but not without a couple of long, involuntary intermissions. The first hall was destroyed in the shelling of the 1848 revolution, the second in the closing stage of World War II. In 1980 an acoustically perfect auditorium was opened; it's concealed behind the restored façade of mid-19th-century Hungarian-Oriental-Moorish style. The list of conductors and performers who appeared in the old Vigadó sums up the history of 150 years of European music: Liszt, Brahms, Wagner, Bartók, Prokofiev, Rubinstein, Heifetz, Casals, Gigli, Björling, von Karajan…

Cruise boats for Budapest sightseeing tours and trips to the Danube Bend leave from the embarkation point at Vigadó tér. In the square between the river and the concert hall stands a marble obelisk engraved simply "1945" and, in Russian and Hungarian, "Glory to the Soviet hero-liberators".

Inland again, **Martinelli tér,** the site of an outdoor market in the 18th century, offers room enough to step back and admire the architecture. The seven-storey building at No. 5 is considered one of Europe's best examples of premodern design. Ceramic tiles ranged in horizontal bands decorate the upper floors in a scheme that was considered revolutionary when the house was completed in 1912. An Art Nouveau building two doors down also catches the eye. It's notable for the mosaic fantasy at roof-line, a patriotic and religious scene surrounded by "3-D" embellishments. The former Servite Church on the square was built in Baroque style in the early 18th century. Martinelli tér also boasts an eastern-bloc rarity: a high-rise parking garage with room for 300 cars.

Just off the square, Budapest's **City Hall** *(Fővárosi Tanács)* fills an entire street in Városház utca. The imposing Baroque building served as a home for Hungarian veterans disabled in the fighting against the Turks. The 19th-century neo-Classical Pest County Hall *(Pest megyei Tanács)* lies just beyond a bend in the same street.

A pedestrians-only shopping street, **Kígyó utca,** runs between Váci utca and the heavy traffic of Felszabadulás tér (Liberation Square). Across all the lanes of cars and buses (but accessible only by pedestrian subway), you can see the refined Baroque lines of a Franciscan church topped by an unexpected neo-Gothic spire. On this site stood a 13th-century church which became a mosque under Turkish rule. Set into the wall of the church, on the Kossuth Lajos utca elevation, is another reminder of the 1838 flood: a sculptural tribute to Baron Miklós Wesselényi, shown standing in a rowboat rescuing people from their rooftops.

A large shop next door to the church, in Károlyi Mihály utca, specializes in religious vestments, candles, statues and icons.

Károlyi Mihály utca contains some distinguished institutions: the Library of the Eötvös Loránd University of Arts and Sciences, the Petőfi Literary Museum, and the university faculties of political science and law (on Egyetem tér). Take a look, too, at **University Church** *(Egyetemi templom)* just off the square in Eötvös Loránd utca. It was built in the 18th century by the Order of St. Paul, the only monastic body of Hungarian origin. The monks themselves fashioned some of the richest wood-carvings inside the church—the stalls, the choir and the Baroque organ, which delights the eyes as much as the ears. The church, bigger within than seems likely from the street, has two graceful towers with bulbous spires in the Budapest style.

In this part of Pest, near the inner boulevard, you stand the best chance of coming upon traces of the medieval city wall. In many cases houses have been built around parts of the wall, so you have to peer into courtyards to find the high crenellated form of Pest's first defences. Some addresses for the archaeological sightseer: 21 Múzeum körút, 28 Magyar utca, 13 Királyi Pál utca, 17 and 19 Bástya utca and 16 Tolbuhin körút.

From Engels Square

An attractive fountain graces Engels tér, one of the busiest squares of Budapest. The fountain, called the Danubius, is crowned by a bearded man symbolizing the Danube. Three female figures below represent tributaries of the mighty river, the Tisza, the Dráva and the Szava. After the war a sprawling intercity coach terminal was built on the square, bringing bustle and diesel fumes to the area.

Deák tér, only a few steps away, straddles all three metro lines. No more apt place could have been chosen for an **Underground Railway Museum** *(Földalatti Vasúti Múzeum);* it is even situated below ground. (The museum entrance is in the pedestrian underpass beneath Tanács Körút.) On view are antiquated and modern metro cars and equipment. Budapest's original underground line, inaugurated in 1896, was the first in continental Europe. It's still in operation, from Vörösmarty tér to Mexikói út, beyond City Park.

Above ground, a new museum adjoins the neo-Classical Evangelical Church building in Deák tér. The National Lutheran Museum *(Evangélikus Országos Múzeum)* contains a valuable collection of old bibles and chalices, plus documents concerning distinguished Protestant statesmen who strongly influenced the history of predominantly Catholic Hungary. The gigantic statue of Martin Luther in the courtyard next door perpetuates the memory of the Reformation leader.

Anker Palace, an overpowering building topped by two domes and a heavy pyramidal roof, dominates the far side of Deák tér. This one-time insurance company headquarters, adorned with a jumble of classical elements, was one of the few structures in Budapest to be left unscathed by the bombs and shells of World War II.

The main avenue leading north, Bajcsy-Zsilinszky út, named after a wartime resistance leader executed in 1944, continues the inner boulevard system. Many of the houses along here are proud examples of the novelties introduced into Budapest architecture at the turn of the century.

The biggest church in Budapest backs onto the boulevard. Construction of the **Basilica** dragged on from 1851 to 1905, long enough to employ three different architects, who chose neo-Classical, Eclectic and neo-Renaissance themes. The formal name of the church is St. Stephen's Parish Church *(Szent István templom)*, but everyone calls it the Basilica,

View of Castle Hill across the Danube: Matthias Church, Hilton Hotel and Fishermen's Bastion.

even though this is an architecturally inaccurate title. King (St.) Stephen I appears in sculptured form above the main portal and on the altar. The dome, now 315 feet high, collapsed in 1868 and needed re-doing. The Basilica is big enough to hold more than 8,000 worshippers, and often does.

Due west of the Basilica, at the Pest end of the Chain Bridge, **Roosevelt tér** honours the wartime U.S. president. The building directly facing the bridge, embellished to the last Art Nouveau detail, is the turn-of-the-century Gresham Palace. On the north side of the square stands the 19th-century neo-Renaissance home of the Hungarian Academy of Sciences. The statue in front depicts Count István Széchenyi (1791–1860), founder of the Academy and the dynamo behind the audacious Chain Bridge project. This first permanent link between the eastern and western halves of Hungary is now called Széchenyi lánchíd, permanently linking the count's name with his brainchild.

Recent construction along the embankment south of Roosevelt tér has restored the area to its pre-war position as a centre of luxury hotels. The first of them was the Duna Intercontinental, followed by the Forum Hotel Budapest and the Atrium Hyatt Hotel. All were built under international agreements. From these hotels, the view across the Danube is priceless: the Citadel, the sprawling palace, the Fishermen's Bastion and the high-flying spire of Matthias Church.

Szabadság tér (Freedom Square), a vast expanse of shade trees and lawns, has its share of monuments, too, including another obelisk dedicated to Soviet soldiers. Official buildings, most of them ostentatious, surround the square. The former Stock Exchange, a showy Eclectic structure, now belongs to Hungarian Television; the Hungarian National Bank headquarters opposite is the work of the same architect.

The **Houses of Parliament** *(Országház)* were built to symbolize the grandeur of the Austro-Hungarian empire. In its day the building was called the biggest in the world. The architect, Imre Steindl (1839–1902), may have had the British parliament on his mind; in any case, the neo-Gothic arches and turrets of Hungary's riverside legislature inevitably remind one of the Westminster style. Out of character, however, is the great dome. At 315 feet, it's the same height as that of the Basilica, putting church and state on an equal plane.

Individual tourists are not admitted to the building, but group excursions are run by the various tour agencies when parliament is not in session. Tourists are escorted into the Assembly Chamber and seated at the desks of members (the left and right sides of the semicircular layout no longer have political significance) to be lectured on how the National Assembly is elected and does its work.

Across Kossuth Lajos tér from the Parliament building, the **Ethnographic Museum** *(Néprajzi Múzeum)* occupies an 1890s building originally meant to be the seat of the Supreme Court (hence the statue of Justice on the façade). The main hall, with its vaulted, frescoed ceiling, is vast enough to serve as a railway station and pompous enough for a royal palace. On permanent display are examples of old-time Hungarian peasant art and culture; textiles, clothing, implements, ceramics and religious icons. As in many Budapest museums, all signs and explanations are printed in Hungarian only.

Beyond the Inner City

Breaking out from the inner city, there are no more ancient monuments—indeed, few buildings more than 150 years old. But the charm of the Pest which expanded so confidently in the 19th and early 20th centuries is hard to resist. Here are the majestic boulevards, the ingeniously decorated apartment blocks, the grand public buildings, the theatres and cafés.

The Little Boulevard (Kiskörút) follows the path of the medieval city wall. The first section starts at the Pest end of Liberty Bridge; it's called Tolbuhin körút (after a Soviet marshal). The road may seem too hectic and businesslike to hold any appeal for sightseers, but the building at No. 1–3 is full of surprises. It's a vast, old-fashioned **covered market**, with a ceiling six stories above the floor, brimming with local colour and exotic smells. This used to be Budapest's central market; now it's an overgrown food bazaar for ordinary shoppers. Don't miss the paprika stalls with their pretty garlands of peppers.

At Kálvin tér the boulevard veers northward along the trajectory of the city wall. The unaffected lines of an early 19th-century Calvinist church stand out, a reminder of the days when this was a quiet, almost rural, crossroads. Kálvin tér has since evolved into one of Budapest's biggest and busiest traffic intersections.

From here the boulevard is called Múzeum körút. It's dominated by the neo-Classical bulk of the **Hungarian National Museum** (*Magyar Nemzeti Múzeum*). This impressive building, with Corinthian columns and richly sculptured tympanum, stands back in its own sizable garden. Inside, amid monumental architectural and ornamental details, the whole story of Hungary unfolds. On display are prehistoric remains and ancient jewels and tools, longbows, locks and keys. From the Turkish era a 17th-century tent is all decked out with carpets on the floor and walls. The 19th-century exhibits range from army uniforms to a piano owned by Liszt, and by Beethoven before him.

For Hungarian visitors, though, there's no argument about which exhibit is the stellar attraction: the Hungarian **royal regalia.** They were returned to Budapest in 1978 after more than three decades in custody in the United States as spoils of war (including a spell in Fort Knox). The crown, attributed to St. Stephen, the great 11th-century king, has more meaning than most. In Hungary it is a powerful symbol of national pride. Also on show are the 11th-century coronation robes, the oriental-style sceptre, the 14th-century gilded orb, and a 16th-century replacement for a ceremonial sword. All are cherished as a supreme national treasure, even more so because of their post-war odyssey.

Beyond the university buildings, the boulevard crosses busy Rákóczi út (named after an 18th-century prince). This is the main east-west avenue of Budapest, and a major shopping street for goods ranging from shoes and antiques to TV sets. Rákóczi út runs straight towards the Eastern Railway Station (*Keleti pályaudvar*) but swerves at the last moment to create a modern plaza with a sunken promenade. The design of the station has been described as Eclectic in style. Statues of James Watt, inventor of the steam engine, and George Stephenson, of the steam locomotive, stand in niches of honour on the façade.

A final curiosity just off the inner boulevard at 2–8 Dohány utca: a mid-19th-century synagogue built in a striking Byzantine-Moorish style. This is the biggest of about 30 synagogues still operating in Budapest. Next door, the **Jewish Religious and Historical Collection** (*Zsidó Múzeum*) contains relics and works of art reflecting many centuries of Jewish life and death in Hungary. Among the exhibits: a 3rd-century gravestone, exquisite medieval prayerbooks and chilling documents on the fate of the Budapest ghetto in World War II.

The Nagykörút

The Great Boulevard (*Nagykörút*) makes a leisurely semicircle about four miles long, embracing all of Pest from Margaret Bridge to Petőfi Bridge. It comprises Szent István körút, Lenin körút, József körút and Ferenc körút. Though it changes names four times, the boulevard has a rather

consistent character—not exceptionally elegant, but full of enthusiasm.

Just off Ferenc körút at 33–37 Üllői út, a building pulsating with architectural shocks houses the **Museum of Applied Arts** (*Iparművészeti Múzeum*). The style of the brick-and-ceramic-tile palace can only be described as Fantasy Hungarian with strong eastern influences. Designed by Ödön Lechner and Gyula Pártos, it was opened in 1896. As for the exhibits, they tell a terse history of ceramics in China, Europe and, in particular, Hungary. Also on show are furniture, textiles, oriental rugs, metalwork, clocks and curios made by extremely talented Hungarian and foreign hands.

A museum of more specialized interest, just beyond the ring of Lenin körút, is the Philatelic Museum (*Bélyegmúzeum*) at 47 Hársfa utca. All the stamps ever issued by Hungary can be viewed here, so there are fascinating historical and human-interest themes.

The long segment of the boulevard now known as Lenin körút has been a traditional centre of Budapest's cultural as well as commercial life. Along here are theatres, cinemas and, less obviously, publishing houses and the haunts of literary and artistic characters. At the boulevard's intersection with Dohány utca, the

73

Hungária Café (formerly known as the New York) looks just as it did when the 20th century was new. The café's astonishing neo-Baroque-Eclectic-Art Nouveau interior has been restored to its original gaudy glory. And once again it's a popular meeting place of actors, writers and nostalgia buffs.

Hungarian folk dancers.

Lenin körút finally runs out at Marx tér, site of the Western Railway Station *(Nyugati pálya-udvar)*. With its high-flying steel framework and cast-iron pillars, this was an architectural sensation of the 1870s. The French firm that built it went on to even greater heights with a daring project in Paris, which was destined to become known as the Eiffel Tower.

Most Stately Avenue

You may never learn how to pronounce the name of **Népköztársaság útja,** but you'll surely admire its harmonious style. Budapest's most attractive avenue, modelled after the Champs-Elysées in Paris, was a bold stroke of the 1870s. The city planners pushed it straight out from the Inner Boulevard to City Park, gradually widening the avenue

along the way and pausing for breath only at a couple of spacious squares.

Népköztársaság útja, meaning People's Republic Avenue, originally was called Sugár út (Radial Avenue). Later it was known as Andrássy út, and for some years it bore Stalin's name. Under whatever title, the avenue has a roomy, patrician feeling. The buildings that line it blend nicely, yet almost every one has unique features—a fountain or statue in the courtyard, a mosaic or frieze on the façade, columns or arches....

The **Postal Museum** *(Postamúzeum)* is tucked away in a large, formerly aristocratic edifice near the beginning of the avenue at 3 Népköztársaság útja. Even if you can't understand the explanations, written in Hungarian only, you will appreciate the rarity of the ancient telephone switchboards, telegraph keys, postboxes, and the telephone of Franz Josef I. On view is the prototype of a revolutionary telegraph transmitter, with the letters of the alphabet assigned to the keys of a piano; but the idea was ahead of its day and won little acclaim at the time.

The **State Opera House** *(Állami Operaház)*, designed by Miklós Ybl, is the most admired piece of architecture on the avenue. Its Italianate style and restrained proportions fit in beautifully with the surroundings. Statues of 16 great opera composers stand high above the entrance; alongside the portico in positions of honour are sculptures of Franz Liszt and his less celebrated contemporary, Ferenc Erkel, composer of the Hungarian national anthem and director of the opera house when it opened in 1884.

The interior design, noted for its pleasing proportions, evinces a general air of great luxury within the bounds of taste. The auditorium, with its splendid four-tiered gallery, provides excellent acoustics. Opera is so popular in Budapest that a second, larger opera house, the Erkel Theatre, was built to ease the pressure for tickets.

Across the avenue from the opera house, in a late 19th-century palace, Hungary's best dancers study at the State Ballet Institute.

An area two or three streets away has suffered the nickname of **Budapest's Broadway.** With the highest concentration of theatres of any single neighbourhood in the capital, as well as the Moulin Rouge nightclub, it's a lively part of town.

The first of the avenue's main intersections, the crossing of Lenin körút, is a bustling place called November 7 tér, commemorating the date of the Bolshevik revolution. Farther from the centre of town the avenue takes

another break at Kodály körönd (circle), named after the composer and educator Zoltán Kodály (1882–1967), who lived here. The curving façades of the buildings ranged around this square are embellished with classical figures and inlaid designs of endless variety.

As the avenue heads out of town, smart villas and mansions in garden settings predominate. Most are now embassies or government offices, but the house at 103 Népköztársaság útja holds the **Museum of East Asian Art** *(Hopp Ferenc Kelet-ázsiai Múzeum).* Ferenc Hopp was an art collector who died in 1919, bequeathing his villa and his hoard of Asian art works to the state. Since then, other collections have been added, bringing the inventory to some 20,000 items. A related institution, the **Museum of Chinese Art** *(Kína Múzeum),* occupies another enviable villa in the same district, at 12 Gorkij fasor. It specializes in ancient Chinese sculpture, ceramics and handicrafts.

Népköztársaság útja ends in an outburst of pomp at Heroes' Square *(Hősök tere),* a wide-open space generously endowed with winter winds. Here stand the statues of patriotic import that form the **Millenary Monument,** begun on the thousandth anniversary of the Magyar conquest. At the heart of the ensemble rises a 118-

foot column supporting a winged figure. Around the pedestal, statues show seven tribal chiefs riding horses. The carved likenesses of historical figures starting with King Stephen I stand in a semicircular colonnade, and there are all the requisite allegorical works as well. In front of this, the stone tablet of the Hungarian War Memorial commemorates the heroes who died for national freedom and independence.

Facing each other across the expanse of Heroes' Square, two neo-Classical structures seem at first glance to be reflections of one another, and indeed they were designed by the same architect. The considerably larger building on the left (north) side is the **Museum of Fine Arts** (*Szépmű- vészeti Múzeum*), an institution of international significance.

On view from ancient times are Egyptian statues and mummy cases, Greek and Roman sculpture and vases. (A note about the Hungarian legends: I.E. 3–1 SZ. = 3rd to 1st century B.C.; I.SZ. 3. SZ = 3rd century A.D.)

The museum's holdings of Old Masters, of which about 600 can be seen at any time, include many sublime works of the Italian Renaissance. An area of unexpected strength is the Spanish school, with seven El Grecos and an ample selection of works by Velázquez, Murillo, Zurbarán and Goya. Many other masters are represented, from Hans Memling and Bruegel the Elder to Frans Hals, Rembrandt and Vermeer. Another surprise is the trove of French Impressionists and Post-Impressionists: Monet, Pissarro, Renoir, Cezanne, Gauguin and others.

Temporary exhibitions of Hungarian and foreign painting and sculpture are held in the Art Gallery (*Műcsarnok*) on the far side of the square. This high-roofed one-storey building was designed in the form of a Greek temple.

Not far from the gallery, Dózsa György út widens to form Procession Square (*Felvonulási tér*). If you like a parade, with plenty of red flags, this is the place to be on Liberation Day (4 April) or May Day. The statue of Lenin is by Pál Pátzay.

The City Park

Beyond the Millenary Monument and all the exaggerated formality sprawls a park where Hungarians can relax, stroll in the woods, spoil their children with ice-cream and cheap plastic toys, hire a rowing boat, even visit another museum.

The City Park (*Városliget*), about 250 acres in area, began to evolve in the early 19th century. Most of the present amenities, such as the artificial lake which reflects the turrets of a make-believe castle, were added during

preparations for the Thousand-Year festivities of 1896.

The **Castle of Vajdahunyad** (*Vajdahunyad vára*) reproduces aspects of the fabulous castle of the Hunyadi family in Transylvania (in an area which became part of Romania). It was built as a prop for the Millenary Exhibition but proved so popular that it was reconstructed in permanent form. One wing of the castle holds the Hungarian Agricultural Museum (*Magyar Mezőgazdasági Múzeum*), which deals with the history of hunting, fishing and farming. There's also a simulated wine cellar displaying old wine presses and bottles; oddly, the place is heated even in summer to protect the exhibits.

In the palace courtyard stands a unique statue of a 13th-century personage known only as Anonymous. He was the royal scribe who wrote the first Hungarian chronicles. A suitably anonymous face peers from deep inside a monk's cowl.

Outside the palace area, another statue shows the American president George Washington looking over a little lake—so far from the Delaware River and the Potomac. It was erected in 1906 by Hungarian émigrés living in the United States.

Sculpted elephants stand guard at the elaborately decorated entrance to the **Zoo** (*Fővárosi Állatkert*). Inside, some 4,000 live ani-

mals stand by to entertain visitors. Most of them are kept in traditional cages, but there are some refreshing exceptions, such as a monkey island in a lake. A hot-house on the zoo grounds displays tropical flora along with some appropriate but unlovely fauna—serpents and crocodiles.

The zoo adjoins **Vidám Park** (Amusement Park), a standard roller-coaster and dodgem establishment. For the foreign tourist, its principal attraction is the chance to watch young Hungarians letting their hair down and having fun. Also here is the municipal Grand Circus *(Fővárosi Nagycirkusz)*.

Across the street lies the overblown triple-domed **Széchenyi Baths,** considered one of Europe's largest medicinal bath complexes. In a spa city like Budapest, it is probably to be expected that piping-hot spring water should bubble under the city park. The Széchenyi installation treats various physical disorders and provides its share of swimming pools.

Near the easternmost point of the park (at 26 Május 1. út), some worthy old trains, planes, cars and motorcycles may be examined in the **Transport Museum** *(Közlekedési Múzeum)*. The exhibits skim the history of transport from the days of sail to the space age. In the museum grounds, an antique railway dining car now serves as a restaurant.

DANUBE BEND

Europe's second-largest river (after the Volga) originates in the Black Forest of Germany. After a journey of 1,776 miles through eight countries it finds the Black Sea. Along the way, the Danube goes under six different names; the Hungarians call it the Duna.

North of Budapest, the river—longer than the Irawaddy, the Orinoco or the Rhine—suddenly changes its mind. It abandons its easterly course for a southerly tack. The scene of this dramatic deviation, known straightforwardly as Dunakanyar, the Danube Bend, shows the river at its most alluring, the lush countryside a delight, the towns aglow with charm. The area is Hungary's prime year-round vacationland, a favourite with hikers and hunters, history buffs and art lovers.

Scarcely 12 miles upstream from Budapest, easily reached by car, bus or suburban railway, is the captivating town of **Szentendre.** Though the area has been inhabited since the Stone Age, the present character of Szentendre remains frozen in the 18th century: tidy, Baroque and painted all the colours of the rainbow. For odd historical reasons, it's unique.

Szentendre first came to notice in the 1st century B.C. under the Illyrians. After the Romans took over, they named it Ulcisia Castra

81

and built fortifications and a civilian settlement. Rampaging Huns, Longobards and Avars followed. By the end of the Dark Ages little was left; the Hungarians who finally settled in the area had to start all over again. They named the hamlet Szentendre (Sanctus Andreas in the 12th-century municipal charter) in honour of St. Andrew, the patron saint of a nearby monastery.

The Serbs, who have given the town its unique character, first arrived in the 15th century as refugees from Turkish military advances in the Balkans. But, like the Hungarians, the newly settled Serbs discovered there was no place to hide from the ambitions of the Ottoman empire. Captured by the Turks, Szentendre became a ghost town. In the late 17th century the Turks were finally expelled from Hungary, but the struggle continued in the Balkans. Serbs, Dalmatians, Bosnians, Albanians and Greeks scrambled northwards, and 800 refugee families made Szentendre their new home. They prospered as merchants and artisans. The faith they brought with them, as well as the wealth they accumulated, may be seen in the rich Orthodox churches with which they surrounded themselves.

In more than 200 years the only thing about Szentendre's main square that has changed is its name. **Marx tér,** as it is now known, so perfectly embodies the spirit of the place and its time that the whole ensemble has been classified as a national historical monument. The cast-iron Rococo cross in the centre of the cobbled square was erected in 1763 by the local Serbian businessmen, thankful that a plague had spared the town.

Danube near Visegrád.

82

The towers of seven churches dominate the Szentendre skyline. The one on Marx tér, a mid-18th-century Baroque church with some Rococo details on the portal and belfry, is known as the **Greek Church;** officially it's the Blago-veštenska Eastern Orthodox Church. Alongside, in what was a schoolhouse in the 18th century, the Ferenczy Museum displays art works of the Hungarian Im-pressionist Károly Ferenczy and his two children.

Other churches of more than routine interest in the town: the Catholic Parish Church, founded in the Middle Ages, with an ancient sundial on the wall; and the Belgrade Church, an 18th-century Greek Orthodox cathedral noted for a richly sculpted ico-nostasis. Around the corner is the entrance to the Collection

of Serbian Ecclesiastical Art (*Szerb Egyháztörténeti gyűjtemény*), where precious icons, carvings and manuscripts have been gathered together.

Of all the museums in this artists' town, the one dedicated to the 20th-century ceramic artist Margit Kovács draws the biggest crowds. Here you'll see attenuated sculptures of wide-eyed damsels and stooped tragic figures in an instantly recognizable style. Opposite the Catholic Parish Church, a smaller museum vibrates with the happy, warm colours of paintings by Béla Czóbel, a much-travelled Hungarian Impressionist who settled in Szentendre.

About 2 miles north-west of town, typical old houses transplanted from the countryside have been assembled at the **Open Air Village Museum** (*Szabadtéri Néprajzi Múzeum*). With its 18th-century timber church and whitewashed thatch-roofed cottages—and not a TV antenna in sight—this simulated "village" provides an ideal setting for historical films, as several producers have noticed.

The museum is also known as Skansen, with a tip of the hat to Stockholm's Skansen, founded in 1891, the world's first attempt to re-create a national way of life. Szentendre's version, a recent innovation, is still growing. The authorities are proud of their 1812 blacksmith's forge, an even older treadmill, and rare old wine presses.

Across the Danube—where the barbarians, after all, held sway in Roman times—there tend to be fewer historical monuments than on the right bank. But one town on the far shore has a character of its own. **Vác** (pronounced to rhyme with American "lots") was a strategic river crossing-point since ancient times; a ferry service still operates. A cathedral stood here in the 11th century, but it fell to the Mongol hordes in 1241; the replacement cathedral fared badly under the Turks. The present **Cathedral** dates from the second half of the 18th century. Half a dozen heroic statues stand on the parapet above the huge Corinthian columns of the façade. Inside, sumptuous frescoes adorn the cupolas and walls. The big paved square in front of the church is devoted to a stark pillar honouring Soviet war heroes. Facing the square are harmonious 18th-century buildings.

Vác has a number of stately squares. The traditional main square, **Március 15. tér,** is a very large triangular plaza occupied by Baroque buildings in assorted colours—red, green, cream and ochre. The building at number 11, the town hall, with a wrought-iron balcony above its front gate, was completed in 1764.

If you follow Köztársaság út

northwards a few streets you will come upon a **triumphal arch** quite out of proportion for a town of about 35,000; the monument was erected in 1764 for a visit to Vác by the Empress Maria Theresa. Considering that the royal tour was the biggest thing that ever happened in Vác, plans were discussed to build a sort of Potemkin village of stage sets to camouflage the otherwise unimpressive parts of the town. But the arch alone, it was finally decided, fulfilled the grandiose requirements.

Back on the right bank of the Danube, a few miles upriver, historic **Visegrád** is set in surpassingly scenic country, where verdant hills come down almost to the water's edge. The strategic importance of this potential bottleneck at a hairpin bend in the river has been evident at least since the 4th century, when the Romans built a fort here.

In the mid-13th century, as Hungary recovered from the destruction of the Mongol invasion, King Béla IV ordered that an impregnable castle be built at Visegrád. The Angevin kings who took power after the House of Árpád died out in 1301 began to transform the castle from a utilitarian stronghold to a palace for imperial pomp. Each succeeding king added a few dozen more rooms until the establishment covered an area now estimated at some 44 acres; and that's only

the building, not counting the grounds around it. Stories of the splendour of Visegrád's **palace** spread across Europe, but in modern times some scholars considered it mostly a myth; after the Turkish occupation and landslides and other disasters, nothing was visibly left. Archaeologists began unearthing the truth of the matter in the 1930s, but they have only brought to light part of the main building.

Most of what remains is left to your imagination, though to give a better idea of the whole palace, some areas have been reconstructed (using obviously new materials to differentiate these sections from the original elements). The terraced palace is dug in, up and down the hillside, part of the landscape.

The ferryboats and hydrofoils from Budapest dock a short distance from the palace, which can be explored at leisure. The public entrance to the palace grounds is through the gate at Fő utca 27. Among the highlights of the five-level structure: the Hercules Fountain (a rare vestige of Hungarian Renaissance architecture), the vaulted galleries of the Court of Honour; and a reconstruction of the Lions' Fountain. A 16th-century archbishop of Esztergom, in a fond recollection of the palace he had visited as a youth, reported that for victory feasts the king ordered wine to

flow from one of the fountains…
"moreover, white and red wine
alternately".

At the edge of town, where the
road from Budapest passes
through the city gate, you can see
the remains of the defences which
stretched all the way up to the
citadel. The round Water Bastion
at riverside was an observation
post. The oldest part of the defence system, called **Solomon's
Tower** *(Salamon tornya),* now
houses the King Matthias
Museum, displaying fragments
and reconstructions of stonework
from the palace. Matthias, the
great 15th-century king, usually
gets the credit for the royal palace, even though he didn't build
it; he only beautified it.

Perched on the very top of the
steep green hill, looking haughty
and invulnerable, is the ancient
citadel. In the summer tourist
season, shuttle buses run from the
King Matthias statue near the city
gate up to the citadel and the
lookout tower of Nagy-Villám.
From the hilltop there are un-
matched views over this most romantic part of the Danube—wide
and tree-lined, with a long, snake-
like green island in the middle.
The river begins its change of
course at the site of **Esztergom,**
cathedral city and medieval capital of all Hungary. In this region
the Danube itself is an international frontier; that's Czechoslovakia on the opposite bank. The

ruins of a bridge which linked the
two countries until World War II
make a melancholy sight from
the heights of Castle Hill.

One of the earliest Magyar rul-
ers, Prince Géza, chose Esztergom as his base. In a grand gesture toward the Holy Roman Empire, the prince announced that
his people would join the western
stream of Christianity. This set
the scene for Esztergom's role as
the ecclesiastical and royal capital
of the young nation.

The great domed **Basilica of
Esztergom** *(Esztergomi Székesegyház),* the biggest church in
Hungary, stands on the site of an
11th-century house of worship. In
1823, shortly after construction
began, Beethoven offered to con-
duct his *Missa Solemnis* for the
consecration of the church. But
the work went too slowly, and
when the ceremony finally took
place, in 1856, it was Liszt's
Esztergom Mass that was performed.

The red-marble side chapel
called the **Bakócz-kápolna,** a pure
example of Italian Renaissance
style, was built as a separate
church in the early 16th century.
It was moved stone by stone to
the basilica in the 19th century
and reassembled. Note the white
marble altar sculpted by a Floren-
tine master. The **treasury** contains
Hungary's richest store of religious
objects, including a 9th-century
cross of crystal from Metz

and the 15th-century Calvary of King Matthias.

Alongside the cathedral the remains of a medieval **royal palace** have been excavated and, to an extent, restored. This is called the oldest stone fortress in Hungary, and the only one to have held out against the 13th-century Mongol siege. Like the Visegrád palace, it was abandoned and forgotten for hundreds of years. Among the highlights: the beautifully-proportioned Royal Chapel, possibly the work of 12th-century French architects and artists; the frescoed Hall of Virtues (listed as Prudence, Temperance, Fortitude and Justice) with the signs of the zodiac on the great arch; and the hall in which, according to tradition, King (later Saint) Stephen was born.

Down at riverside, Esztergom's **Christian Museum** *(Keresztény Múzeum)* is rated the most important provincial collection in Hungary. It definitely comes up to world standards, especially in its supply of superb 14th- and 15th-century Italian paintings. Housed in the former Episcopal Palace, the museum is run by the Catholic Church and subsidized by the state. Elsewhere in the building are photographs of some of the churches, some 170 in all, built in Hungary since 1945.

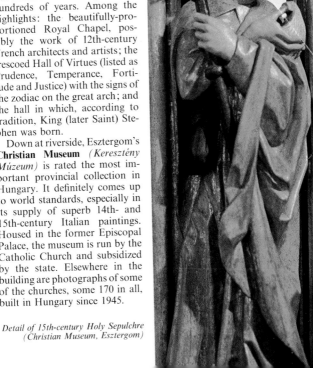

Detail of 15th-century Holy Sepulchre (Christian Museum, Esztergom)

WESTERN BORDER REGION

The wooded hills along the frontier with Austria have been called the Hungarian Alps. As they never attain an altitude of even 3,000 feet, this might seem some sort of Hungarian joke. But in fact they are foothills of the authentic Alps of Austria, and much appreciated as recreational assets. But whether or not you take these hills seriously, the towns of the western border region live up to all requirements in the realms of history, art and unforgettable charm.

Sopron (population more than 50,000) is a delightful ancient walled town surrounded by pleasant modern additions, 6 kilometres from the Austrian border. The beauty of the setting may be seen from afar, from the flat-roofed observation tower on Károly-magaslat (Károly Heights). The air is cool and clear, and the view down onto treetops and beyond to the town and Lake Fertő is a thoroughly refreshing aside.

The Romans called Sopron Scarbantia and made it an important junction on the Amber Road linking Byzantium with Vindobona (now Vienna). The elliptical shape of today's town centre is identical with that of the Roman

Eszterházy Palace at Fertőd.

walled town; the main temple to the ancient gods was built where the town council building stands today. It is almost impossible to dig anywhere under the streets or houses of Sopron without coming upon a statue, gravestone, remnant of the original city wall or the municipal water system of the Romans.

Sopron's most visible landmark, the **Fire Tower** *(Tűztorony)*, is a bit like an archaeological exercise, but above the ground; the newest is on top, of course. The tower is made of three parts: the thick, round bottom portion, the thinner, octagonal superstructure, and the slim topmost tower. The lowest element was a medieval adaptation of the original city gate of the Romans. The next stage, built in the 16th century, reflects dignified Renaissance style. The bulbous topping is 17th-century Baroque.

It's 124 steps up to the observation level of the tower, from which the panorama of the steep tiled roofs of the old town is thoroughly endearing. The houses may seem haphazardly arranged, but they fit well inside the ancient ramparts.

You have to pay an admission fee to climb the tower, but this includes a visit to the basement alongside—a **museum** of Roman relics found on the site. Statuary, amphorae, vials, vases and jewellery are all in first-class repair.

But except for one box of old Roman coins, the numismatic effects in the display cases come from mischievous student visitors, who slip modern Hungarian forints behind the glass.

The base of the tower is pierced by the Gate of Loyalty, linking the outer and inner town. Though the gate appears to be a historic construction, it is actually a 20th-century commemoration of this border town's long record of dedication to Hungary. Walking through the gate (pedestrians only) into old Sopron, you find yourself in the main square, **Fő tér,** surrounded by historic buildings. But there is little solemnity in this living museum, brightened by outdoor cafés and flocks of pigeons and children.

The Trinity Statue in the middle of the square was erected in 1701; except for the present City Hall, most of the buildings here are 15th-century treasures. The City Hall, which looks rather like an opera house because of its arcaded façade, holds the municipal archives, including rare medieval documents.

Among the sights on the square are the small **Patika Múzeum** at No. 2 Fő tér, a pharmacy with all the centuries-old furnishings and equipment preserved; the **Gambrinus House** at No. 3, which served as the city hall in the Middle Ages; and the arcaded **Fabricius House** at No. 6. The latter, now a museum, is furnished as an aristocratic 18th-century town house. Behind the Fabricius House, look for the rather run-down stairway to a cellar containing Roman statues and inscriptions, found on the site or elsewhere around Sopron. Next door, at No. 7, a small museum highlights 17th- and 18th-century stonework—statues, seals, escutcheons and decorations.

The Gothic church on Fő tér is called **Kecske-templom,** meaning Goat Church. Goats appear on the crests carved on the building. A popular legend says the money to build the church came from a medieval goatherd whose livestock had stumbled upon gold. The original 13th-century church was expanded and modernized over hundreds of years.

On the opposite side of the square, the corner building at No. 8, the **Storno House,** is one of Sopron's most stylish buildings. The late Renaissance palace, with added Baroque elements, has housed such distinguished and varied guests as King Matthias and Franz Liszt.

To appreciate the overall atmosphere of old Sopron, explore the quiet cobbled streets from one surprise to the next: medieval and Baroque buildings in diverse designs and colours. Some of the buildings which look relatively modern have had parts of their

Ancient quarry at Fertőrákos.

front walls stripped bare to the Gothic innards, like x-rays of their architectural pedigree. When it comes time to pause in the sightseeing you'll be happy to notice a scattering of genuine old wine cellars, some done up appealingly. They offer snacks and the chance to taste the local wines.

In Új utca, meaning New Street, the traces of a 14th-century synagogue may be glimpsed at No. 11. At No. 22, another medieval house serves as a museum with a reconstruction of parts of another old synagogue and some historic religious artefacts on show.

Szent György utca, essentially parallel to Új utca, contains the

Erdődy Palace (No. 16), an early Rococo gem. The Eggenberger House, at No. 12, is notable for its arcaded courtyard.

The main street of Sopron, Lenin körút, curves around the outside of the town wall. Many historic houses still stand in this street, including the old White Horse Inn at No. 55; among its clients was the composer Joseph Haydn.

Another composer with strong local connections, Franz Liszt, made his debut as a child prodigy pianist in Sopron. Records of his life and career, portraits and manuscripts are contained in the Sopron museum named after him, the **Liszt Ferenc Múzeum,** set in its own little park in Május 1. tér (May 1 Square). You have to ring the bell to be admitted; you then don felt overshoes to protect the floor. The museum's principal exhibits are devoted to documenting the life of Sopron over the centuries, with examples of clothing, utensils, furniture, weapons… and the fruits of local intellectual pursuits.

Back in Lenin körút, you could easily miss seeing Sopron's most humble superlative. The house at No. 42 contains what is

Countryside around Pannonhalma.

claimed to be the smallest shop in Hungary, a watchmaker's establishment barely wider than its narrow front door.

Sopron is a convenient base for excursions throughout the northwest border region, a district strong on historical and natural attractions.

Among the most unusual sights—here or anywhere—is the ancient quarry at **Fertőrákos,** less than 10 kilometres from the heart of Sopron. On the edge of this border village, the Romans began extracting stone to build their houses and tombs. The operations continued for centuries, leaving colossal halls carved into the hill-

sides—not like a tunnel or coal mine but lofty caverns with everything at right angles.

Grass now covers the centre of the man-made crater; further excavations go off to the side. From the walkway, which looks down on the digs, you can also survey the surrounding countryside: hilly forests to one side, marshy borderland to the other (beyond the frontier watch-towers on the skyline lies Austria).

You can go deep inside one of the galleries. The ceilings are so high that you're scarcely likely to get claustrophobia. The subterranean hall is so spacious that it is used as the setting for operas and Greek tragedies during Sopron Festival Weeks. A full-scale theatre has been set up inside the cavern, with a modern stage, professional lighting equipment, and comfortable seats for the audience.

These excavations were last used for more prosaic purposes during World War II. Old-timers recall that the Germans, taking advantage of the quarry's immunity from air attack, turned it into an underground aircraft factory.

A kiosk on the site sells seashells which were found embedded in the rock of the quarry, sold with a guarantee: none less than five million years old!

Lake Fertő, comprising part of the Austro-Hungarian border (it's the Neusiedler See on the other side), is off-limits to foreigners here but a popular recreation area for residents of the Sopron area. The alkaline, saltwater lake and its surrounding boglands attract more than 250 species of waterfowl. The water and mud of the lake are said to have therapeutic value.

The water flowing from mineral springs at nearby **Balf,** rich in hydrogen sulphide, has been used for rheumatism and back problems since the time of the Romans. Nowadays a luxurious spa-hospital operates in a park containing an 18th-century chapel. Balf's popularity with foreign patients is easy to understand: for the price of a mere motel room in some other country, the guests enjoy tasteful accommodation, meals included, the services of a polyglot medical staff, and all the healthful H_2O they can drink and bathe in. The resources here are not limited to water: vineyards come right down the hillside to the spa.

Fertőd, a hamlet 27 kilometres east of Sopron, used to be named Eszterháza, after the princely family which chose that spot for a palace, park and game preserve. After long neglect followed by the damage of World War II, the parks and gardens are being rehabilitated; the château itself has been transformed from a ruin to its original baroque gloss. You'll soon understand why the

Palace of Fertőd has always been known as the Hungarian Versailles.

As eras are counted, the golden age of Fertőd lasted but an instant—from the late 1760s to 1790. These were the years when Miklós Eszterházy enjoyed the title, wealth and power of Prince of the Holy Roman Empire. He converted an undistinguished hunting headquarters into an imperial palace, which he proceeded to fill with art, culture and gaiety.

The 126-room palace holds a special appeal for music lovers, for Miklós the Magnificent had the good taste to hire Joseph Haydn as his composer-in-residence and all-round musical functionary. The first stop on the guided tours of the establishment is the grand, gilt music room, one of the places where Haydn and his musicians performed. Copies of his manuscripts and string instruments of the epoch are on show.

Every month a new opera was produced at Eszterháza. The opera house specially constructed for Haydn burned down in the 19th century. The prince and his guests sat in boxes and galleries while opera lovers of other classes occupied about 400 seats downstairs. Of course, it was all free of charge; a prince could hardly sell tickets. Haydn's operas were also put on in the nearby Puppet Theatre. The theatre building has been totally revamped over the years; today, unrecognizable, it serves as one of the palace outbuildings.

The horseshoe-shaped palace is approached through a wrought-iron Rococo gate. The façade of the central section is rich in original details: twin ceremonial staircases, lamps held by cherubs, vases, and windows in varied shapes and sizes.

Inside, the Music Room and the Banquet Hall, back to back, are the biggest, tallest (two stories) and most lavishly appointed rooms. But all the rooms restored since the war flaunt the original air of Rococo luxury. Notice the chandeliers, the ceramic stoves (a different design in each room), panelled walls, frescoed ceilings, parquet floors. To protect the flooring, visitors are required to wear felt overshoes, provided at the entrance.

A stately home of less formidable proportions may be visited at **Nagycenk,** where Routes 84 and 85 converge south-east of Sopron. Whereas Fertőd was a prince's palace, the two-storey mansion at Nagycenk was the seat of a count. The estate is closely linked with the life of Count István Széchenyi, a pacesetter in 19th-century Hungary's political and intellectual life. On a practical plane, the count installed gas lights in this house before anyone else in the country had them. He also introduced what may well have been Hungary's first flush toilets and running-water bathtubs. Széchenyi, however, is more widely remembered for sponsoring Budapest's Chain Bridge and founding the Hungarian Academy of Sciences.

The history of this influential family is documented in a memorial museum within the imposing white mansion. One wing of the building has been turned into a small hotel with—appropriately—all modern conveniences.

Nagycenk's formal gardens, begun more than two centuries ago, are famous for the two-mile-long avenue of linden trees. Nearby, the Széchenyi Museum Railway, where ancient steam engines survive, is popular with narrow-gauge enthusiasts and wide-eyed children. The line links Nagycenk and the village of Fertő-boz a couple of miles away.

Kőszeg is a quiet old walled town with many of the historic buildings brightly redecorated. For much of the way from Nagycenk to Kőszeg the road parallels the Austrian border. The frontier's proximity obviously affected the history of Kőszeg, the scene of many a battle between Austrian and Hungarian armies. In the early 18th century the town changed hands a number of times.

But the most unforgettable battle for Kőszeg was a one-sided struggle enacted in 1532. With the forces of the Ottoman empire at the gates, the garrison in the Kőszeg castle held out for more than three weeks. The way the Hungarians tell it, the odds were 200,000 Turks to about one-thousand defenders. By delaying the Ottoman advance and exhausting the energies of the invasion force, it is said, the sacrifice of the Kőszeg garrison saved Vienna.

The hero of the siege of Kőszeg was Captain Miklós Jurisich, whose name you will see on all sides of the town today. Jurisich Square, the centre of the walled town, is reached through Hősi kapu (Heroes' Gate), which is dedicated to Captain Jurisich and his men. The arched passageway cuts through a tall, historic-looking tower which proves to have been built in 1932, commemorating the siege's 400th anniversary.

Within and without the town walls, Kőszeg (population about 12,000) maintains an unhurried, rural pace. There is no rush about inspecting the historic churches and civic buildings; take time to notice the careful decorative touches on the fronts of the houses... or sniff the flowers.

Most of the town's outstanding buildings are grouped around the large **main square** *(Jurisich tér)*. On the façade of the Town Hall (at No. 8), religious frescoes and heraldry alternate with the windows of the main floor; the build-

Romanesque church and chapel at Ják.

ing dates from the 14th century. The General's House *(Tábornok-ház)* at No. 6, built in the 17th century, consolidated two earlier houses. Other buildings on the square are embellished with *sgraffiti*—floral or geometric designs.

Two historic churches stand side by side in the square. **St. Emerich's** *(Szent Imre-templom)* is a 17th-century Baroque church with some Gothic and Renaissance touches. **St. James'** *(Szent Jakab-templom),* next door, is a couple of centuries older; look for the 15th-century frescoes on the right front wall.

An easy, direct way to get to the castle is to follow Rájnis utca, which leads northwestwards from the main square. Notice this street's row of houses set in a saw-tooth pattern, still an attractive idea although the original purpose—enhancing defensive fields of gunfire—is no longer a factor.

The **castle** was built in the 14th century. Like most buildings of that age, it was submitted to periodic reconstruction and repairs, which explains the added Renaissance and Baroque elements. Aside from its importance as a historical relic, the castle serves several active functions: as the local House of Culture, the site of a museum, and, less predictably, a tourist hostel and a coffee-shop-cum-disco. And another light touch: part of the moat surrounding the castle (it's all dried out these days) now serves as a children's playground.

The castle's modern **museum** contains an enviable collection of ceremonial swords and decorative rifles from the 17th and 18th centuries as well as less glamorous old weapons. The original municipal charter and other historical documents may be seen along with local handicrafts. Inside the castle grounds stands a statue of Captain Jurisich, the defender.

Szombathely, with a population greater than 80,000, is the biggest of the Hungarian towns along the Austrian border. Although it's a busy commercial and industrial centre, bicycles are still a prime means of transport inside the town—and a good way to attack the parking problem.

What puts Szombathely on the tourist map is its historical distinction. Szombathely claims to be the oldest town in Hungary, and shows off some ancient ruins to prove it. The Roman Emperor Claudius gave it colonial status in A.D. 43, under the name of Savaria. Sixty-four years later it became the capital of all Upper Pannonia. But like most Hungarian towns, it suffered a generous share of cruel reverses over the centuries, the most serious in 1241 when the Mongol hordes burned down everything in sight.

In the late 1950s researchers dug up Savaria's rarest relics: the **ancient sanctuary** of the Egyptian goddess Isis. The stone columns have been patched back together but still stand, and they serve as a classical backdrop for operas and concerts every summer. Alongside and above the "digs", remnants of provincial Roman civilization are displayed in a small museum building. Most of the items—pottery, glass, utensils—have been damaged in one way or another, but seeing them on the original site compensates for their imperfections.

The Iseum is only one of Szombathely's archaeological attractions. Behind the Cathedral, important traces of Roman and medieval culture are unearthed in the **Garden of Ruins** (*Romkert*). There is a 20-yard-long mosaic floor in a moderately good state of preservation, as well as coins and other portable relics. The shape of the ancient Christian Basilica of St. Quirinus is disclosed by its foundation stones. And you can walk the big black slabs of the Amber Road, the Roman trade route that once ran all the way from Constantinople to the Baltic.

The neo-Classic Catholic **Cathedral,** big enough to hold 5,000 worshippers, was begun at the end of the 18th century. A raid by U.S. Air Force bombers in March, 1945, all but destroyed the building, but it has been fully restored. The adjacent square, Berzsenyi tér, is the site of the elegant Episcopal Palace, in late Baroque style. Across the square, at No. 1, is the County Hall, with the Small Town Hall alongside.

A few streets east, at No. 9 Kisfaludy Sándor utca, the **Savaria Museum** devotes its ground floor to Hungarian paintings. But the basement is filled with significant Roman stonework finds: statues, sarcophagi and stone tablets uncovered in Szombathely. Gravestones, it seems, haven't changed much in 2,000 years, though some of the old Roman versions are adorned with charming sculptural details.

If the centre of Szombathely is too businesslike to be very appealing, the parks and recreational facilities of the peripheral areas considerably brighten the scene. On the northern edge of town, the **Arboretum** has 2,000 species of trees and shrubs, and a country calm disturbed only by the playful cries of coachloads of schoolchildren and the calls of the whippoorwills. In a rose garden you'll find flowers named after Queen Elizabeth, Maria Callas, Sophia Loren and the original Eve. Otherwise, everything here goes by its Latin name.

Hungary is full of villages whose names are longer than their main streets—daunting names like Agyagosszergény and Zempléni-hegység. And then there is **Ják**. No signposts advertise Ják, but it's worth getting lost looking for this tiny, pious village 10 kilometres beyond the southern city limits of Szombathely. (On the way out of Szombathely on Route 86, turn right in suburban Perint at Néphadsereg utca, then follow the curving unnumbered road through green fields alternating with thick forests.) The scenery is a balm to the harried traveller. Suddenly the flat horizon reveals the twin towers of Ják's hilltop church, an architectural treasure of world importance.

The Romanesque **church** of the Benedictine monastery of Ják was consecrated in 1256. Disasters big and small have befallen the church—the Mongol invasion during its construction, the Ottoman occupation, a bull's-eye lightning strike. It was restored less than a century ago, not long after its architectural significance had been reappraised.

Although the three-storey towers appear to be identical, other elements of the design are just slightly askew. For instance, only the north tower has a rose window, and the arches over the exquisitely carved main portal are minutely asymmetrical. Nonetheless, the whole of the church inspires an impression of total harmony.

The **sculptures** around the main entrance are admired as Hungary's greatest Romanesque stonework, although the heads of most of the apostles were lost—perhaps in Turkish times—and replaced in Baroque style. Researchers believe the original stone-carvers were Hungarians who finally migrated to Austria, where their work has been traced. Inside the two-aisled church, other sculptural and architectural touches are worth close examination, as well as 13th-century murals portraying, most recognizably, St. George and the dragon.

Alongside the church is a tall white chapel with a floor plan resembling a four-leaf clover and a wood-shingled onion-dome. Szent Jakab-kápolna (Chapel of St. James) once served as the parish church.

One final city of western Hungary is hard to overlook: it's right on the main highway almost exactly halfway between Vienna and Budapest. **Győr** is a cheerful riverside town, strong on heavy industry but a tourist attraction as well.

Because of its strategic location, Győr has made history over many centuries. The Romans called it Arrabona. In the 13th century the city won the right to tax traffic in transit. By the 19th century only Budapest surpassed

Győr as a Hungarian grain marketing centre. But industry soon eclipsed trade as the economic strong-point and today the city is best known as a manufacturer of trains and trucks.

As befits a dynamic city of more than 125,000 people, Győr is pervaded by modern buildings, though the historical monuments are all around. Among the eye-catching new structures is the Kisfaludy Opera House, named after the local poet and playwright Károly Kisfaludy (1788–1830). The theatre's roof curves like a ski-jump, with the stage beneath the highest point; bold abstract designs in tile decorate the sides of the marble-and-glass structure.

A shockingly modern glass building, mercifully low-lying, has been planted immediately next to the ancient Cathedral, muddling the mood in historic Martinovics Square. The **Cathedral** itself, however, has gone through just about every phase of architecture between the 11th century, when it was founded, and the 19th. The essentially Gothic church was rebuilt in Baroque style in the 17th century; the neo-Classic façade was tacked on 200 years later; and then the damage incurred during World War II had to be repaired. The chapel dedicated to St. Ladislas, among the oldest parts of the cathedral, contains a reliquary considered a masterpiece of Hungarian goldsmith's art. Other works of gold, silver, copper and enamel, as well as ceremonial vestments, may be seen in the Cathedral's treasury.

Around the cathedral, winding streets of the area called Káptalan-domb (Chapter Hill) are full of historic atmosphere: the medieval keep, the Bishop's Palace, and remains of the town bastions along the river.

Two other churches of which Győr is particularly proud:

The **Carmelite Church** *(Karmelita templom)* in Köztársaság tér (once known as Carmelites' Square) is a Baroque achievement of the early 18th century. The gracefully proportioned façade has statues in three niches and a large window in the organ loft. Rich paintings and carvings decorate the interior. Incidentally, nearly all the buildings facing this square are prized historic monuments.

In Széchenyi tér, a couple of streets to the east, the **Jesuit Church** (later Benedictine) was built in the 17th century; the façade came afterwards, the bell towers still later. There are three chapels on each side of the nave. The furnishings, frescoes and statues are noteworthy.

Opposite, the Baroque house at 5 Széchenyi tér contains the **János Xantus Museum,** named after a 19th-century scholar. Well displayed are Roman glassware, swords of the Asian hordes who subdued Győr in the 6th century, early Magyar implements, Turkish weapons and a hand-painted Koran, and later Hungarian relics — in sum, a documentary history of the town and its fortunes.

Strolling through the historic heart of the town today, in pedestrians-only streets plentifully supplied with outdoor cafés, you might well agree with the local promoters that it all turned out rather nicely in the end.

Pannonhalma, about 20 kilometres south-east of Győr, is a historic hilltop monastery which still functions as a church-run secondary school with monks as well as lay teachers. The establishment is a treasure-house of architectural and artistic accomplishments; its 300,000-volume library is a scholar's joy.

The story of Pannonhalma goes back to the age of Prince Géza (972–997), the first Magyar leader to embrace Christianity. During his reign Benedictine monks first settled on this hill. The monastery's archives preserve a document, dated 1001, in which Géza's son, King (Saint) Stephen, acknowledges the institution's lands and privileges. But major construction of the monastery didn't begin until the 13th century, and much of the complex belongs to the last century.

The **Abbey Church** was rebuilt in the 19th century upon early medieval foundations. The oldest part of the church, the crypt, is laid out with three naves. According to tradition, the abbot's chair next to the west wall was a throne of King Stephen. The entrance from the medieval cloister to the church, called the *porta speciosa,* is a colourfully decorated portal of red marble and white limestone; you can still decipher graffiti carved in the pedestal by 16th-century "tourists"—if you can read Latin!

The monastery's small art gallery is packed with paintings, the best known being *Fête in Brussels* by David Teniers. This merry 17th-century scene stands out amongst the religious themes of the other Italian, German and Dutch masters on show.

Called the largest of all the world's Benedictine libraries, the T-shaped **library** has high vaulted ceilings, and walls filled with rare books. Beautiful illuminated manuscripts, old maps, bibles and historic documents are displayed. On one wall is a copy of the deed to the abbey at Tihany, on Lake Balaton; dated 1055, it is the first official document to use Hungarian words interspersed in the Latin text. The original is kept in the library's manuscript archives, which guard much of the nation's history.

Trinity Statue (1701) on main square, Sopron.

LAKE BALATON

Hungary's favourite summer vacationland is only 100 kilometres south-east of Budapest: Lake Balaton, Central Europe's biggest lake.

Deprived of a seacoast, Hungarians take their solace by swimming, fishing, sailing and just loafing in this freshwater haven. Balaton is surrounded by a little world of varied beauty comprising fertile plains and abrupt hills, orchards and vineyards, and villages with historic churches and whitewashed thatched cottages.

The lake's area is nearly 230 square miles, or slightly bigger than the Lake of Geneva. But whereas Lake Geneva goes down to a depth beyond 1,000 feet, the average depth of Balaton is a modest 10 feet. This is the shallow secret of Balaton's mild summer temperatures and prolonged bathing season. It also explains why the lake freezes so early (in December), to the delight of local ice-fishermen. Fishing through a hole in the ice has been popular here since antiquity, for winter was the only season when the catch could be preserved for sale in distant parts.

In summer, fishermen—mostly amateurs—operate from shore, from boats, and lounging on platforms protruding from the lake. About 40 species of fish thrive in Balaton; pike-perch *(fogas)* is often singled out as the tastiest of all. Some giant pike-perch weigh in at 20 pounds.

The lake's mineral content—plenty of calcium and magnesium, for instance—is said to have a therapeutic effect on swimming bodies of the human species. As in other countries, however, the problem of pollution has surfaced, mostly at Balaton's western end, and efforts are underway to upgrade the quality of the water. But the cloudy colour may be explained by perfectly innocent chemical and physical phenomena.

Geologists have discovered that the lake is a relatively new feature of the countryside—a mere 20,000-odd years old—which would mean that the pre-historic people who lived here during the ice age were deprived of the lake's recreational benefits. By the time of the Romans, Balaton was a popular area because of the medicinal spas around its shores, some still flourishing. But the idea of swimming for fun in Lake Balaton (or any other lake or river) didn't catch on until the 19th century. Resort hotels, camping sites, sun-tan oil and bikinis came later.

Now for a survey of points of greatest interest around the lake, starting counter-clockwise from the eastern (Budapest) end. After covering the lakeside towns and

villages, we note some historic "inland" places within easy striking distance of resort towns. The only complication is the nomenclature: a couple of dozen of the towns have names beginning "Balaton", muddying the waters for new arrivals. Balatonakarattya, for example, is the first town on Highway 71, the north shore road. Then comes Balatonkenese, and so forth. Some of the names can barely be squeezed onto the road signs.

A Flare for Storms

The wind is taken very seriously indeed at Lake Balaton, where waves 6 feet high can develop.

Since storms often arrive unexpectedly, the authorities operate a last-minute warning service. When yellow rockets are fired, boats must come close to the shore. Red rockets, meaning winds above 38 miles per hour, order everybody snappily out of the water.

The odds are good, though, that you'll never see Balaton all churned up. Statistics show there are only 15 to 20 really tempestuous storms in any one average year.

Balatonalmádi, a fast-growing resort town, claims to have the biggest, most modern beach on the north shore—"capacity 12,000". Parks, hotels and a complete shopping centre round out the picture.

The informal resort of Alsóörs has two unusual monuments in its park. One is a memorial to Soviet pilots who crashed at this spot during World War II. The other commemorates the steamship traffic founded on Lake Balaton in 1846; the inventive Count István Széchenyi started the service with a 40-horsepower boat. Up the hill a 16th-century stone house is known locally as the Turkish House. It seems to have no connection with the Ottoman occupation of Hungary; rather, the shape of the chimney reminds people of a turbaned head, thereby giving the place its name.

Westward, **Balatonfüred** is a busy pleasure port with a long history as a spa. The local mineral water is dispensed to the public from a pagoda-like well-head in the middle of Gyógy tér (Therapeutic Square). It's cool enough to be refreshing, but the taste—as if the pipe were rusty—hints at its medicinal properties. The Heart Hospital, facing the square, treats some 10,000 patients per year. Before Balatonfüred's mineral water was found to help the treatment of heart diseases, the spa specialized in kidney and stomach ailments, and later lung problems. Between the square and the lakefront, a large park shaded by tall plane and poplar trees is studded with statues traditional and modern. The subjects range from *Girl Playing Lute* to *The Fisherman* and *The Ferryman,* right alongside the water, to *Balaton Wind* on the pier.

The **Tihany peninsula**, largely given over to a national park, protrudes to within about a mile of the south shore. Life here is a split-level affair—an ancient church stands on a precipice overlooking the port, and at intermediate altitudes there's a village and an independent lake.

Starting at the top: the **Abbey Church** *(Apátság),* an 18th-century Baroque construction, rises above a crypt nearly a thousand years old. Here stands the tomb of King Andrew I, founder of this Benedictine abbey. In a country ravaged by so many invasions, the Romanesque crypt represents a rare survival from the earliest times of the Hungarian nation. King Andrew is also commemorated in a joltingly contemporary sculpture in front of the church— a stone figure wrapped in an aluminium cloak.

The **Tihanyi Museum,** occupying the Baroque monastery building alongside the church, deals with the history of the region from the Roman epoch to the tourist era. In the basement is a display of ancient Roman stonework and parts of mosaic floors.

The streets and lanes along the upper reaches of **Tihany** town charm visitors. They're lined with thatch-roofed, stone cottages in traditional style. The thatch is a local product; the reeds grow profusely in the lake along the northern shore, helping to keep the water pure as well as adding to the mood of Balaton. In winter the crop stands conveniently above the solid ice to allow for easy harvesting.

At an altitude of more than 80 feet above Lake Balaton, the peninsula's Inner Lake *(Belső-tó)* yields tons of fish every year. Because it is so small—less than half a mile long—the green hills surrounding the little lake look like real mountains. To the south are the domes of defunct geysers.

Beyond Tihany the north coast traffic thins out, so travellers can relax and enjoy the views, vineyards and villages. The region of **Badacsony** produces notable wines on hillsides of volcanic soil. The volcanic past is evident at first sight of the astonishing conical green hills arrayed here. The black basalt slabs used to pave the back roads provide another clue to the violent birth of this land. The view up to the evocative Badacsony mountains is a highspot of an excursion to Lake Balaton; so is the panorama from the top, with the vineyards sloping down to the lake in regimented rows. The next step is obvious: sample the local pride. The wine always tastes better when you're beside the vines.

105

The road moves inland after Badacsony, skirting the ancient village of Szigliget, watched over by the moody remains of a medieval fortress. Thanks to its position at the top of a steep hill almost surrounded by lake and swamp, the 13th-century **fortress of Szigliget** turned out to be impregnable. Even the Turkish armies couldn't dislodge its defenders. But the Habsburgs demolished all but a few walls of the castle complex in an unsentimental 18th-century clean-up campaign.

At the western end of the lake, the town of **Keszthely** used to be owned lock, stock and barrel by one family—the Festetics. The 101-room **Festetics Palace** is one of Hungary's important Baroque monuments. Count György Festetics founded Europe's first agricultural school, now Keszthely's University of Agricultural Sciences, in 1797. He also amazed townspeople by building the *Phoenix*, the biggest ship seen on Balaton till then, a three-master powered with help from 24 oarsmen. Keszthely's **Balaton Museum** surveys the lake from many viewpoints—geology, biology, history and ethnology. Note the curious fossils called "Bela's goat hooves"; legend has it that Bela IV had to drown his flock here when fleeing before the Mongols.

Badacsony vineyards.

Many of the items on display in the Balaton Museum come from an archaeological site 8 kilometres south of Keszthely on Route 71. The ruins of Fenékpuszta are now surrounded by a park. In Roman times this was a fortified town called Valcum. In the 5th century, invaders from the east overran the place, but its prosperity seems to have continued during the Dark Ages. Relics of the Goths, Huns and Avars have been found here.

The highway continues around the end of the lake to the first town on the south shore. This road and rail junction has a folk museum and the longest name: Balatonszentgyörgy. To the west lies Kis-Balaton (Little Balaton), a national reserve noted for its rare birdlife. Ornithologists have counted 80 species of birds among the reeds here, including cormorants, great crested grebes, and, most prized, the white egret. To let the birds nest in peace the area is closed to the public, but serious birdwatchers may apply for permission to visit. The organization to write to is the National Board for Environment and Nature Protection *(Országos Környezet- és Természetvédelmi Hivatal)*, Költő utca 21, H-1121 Budapest.

East of Balatonszentgyörgy, when the highway (now Route 7) finally comes in sight of the lake, Balaton's endless children's beach begins. All along the south

107

shore the soft, white sandy bottom of the lake goes out seemingly to infinity before the water becomes deep enough to dive into. However, this is no problem for sailing, board-sailing (windsurfing), or simply paddling about. To protect the lake from oil- and noise-pollution, the authorities have banned motorboats, and hence water-skiing.

One of the quieter resorts, Balatonmáriafürdő, has almost 6 miles of beach. The town was first settled by farmers from other parts of the region who had lost their grapevines to the 19th-century epidemic of phylloxera. They found the sandy soil around Balatonmáriafürdő more resistant to the disease. Nowadays the emphasis is on holiday homes, not agriculture, but the local wines are still highly regarded.

A volcanic hill with twin peaks hangs over **Fonyód,** the centre of a string of south coast resorts. On the taller peak, called Castle Hill *(Várhegy),* earthen defences were built in the Iron Age. Fonyód's harbour is one of Balaton's main maritime installations. Long after the bathers have packed up, fishermen stake out the unusually long pier and surrounding beaches. Inland, the remains of a 16th-century border fort are surrounded by a system of moats. The terrain here was so marshy that the Turkish army never managed to get round

to capturing the Fonyód fort.

At Szántód the lake is squeezed to its narrowest—less than a mile across, with the Tihany peninsula just over the way. This has always been a vital ferry station. Until as recently as 1928 the ferries were propelled by oarsmen, six men to a boat, with the crossing a 45-minute job in good weather and up to two hours if it involved fighting wind and waves. The modern ferryboats, diesel powered, traverse the strait in less than ten minutes, but there's still plenty of nautical excitement and fresh air. Ferries and pleasure boats stop at many Balaton ports but the route between Szántód and Tihany has the only car ferries on the lake.

The largest town on the south coast, **Siófok,** boasts a beach with room for tens of thousands of sunbathers and a harbour big enough to shelter all the ferries and cruise ships on the lake. A shady recreational park stretches east from the port and winds up in a development of lake-front hotels. Around the harbour a lively assortment of cafés, bars, restaurants and entertainment facilities stand within easy reach.

In the 3rd century, Roman engineers built the first canal at Siófok to divert excess water from the lake. The Sió canal leads all the way from the harbour to the River Danube, down near the Yugoslav frontier.

'Inland' from Balaton

Fortress of Sümeg.

Well within an hour's drive of Lake Balaton are half a dozen towns definitely worth visiting, whether you're spending your holidays on the lake or touring the country.

The biggest and oldest of these towns is **Székesfehérvár** (population more than 100,000), founded about a thousand years ago in a swampy region of central Transdanubia. Nearby is Lake Velence (Velencei-tó), a sort of mini-Balaton. The town's marshy inaccessibility was its strong point during all the invasions and disasters that jolted Hungarian history. To this day Székesfehérvár seems an out-of-the-way place; it's only a few miles off the motorway linking Budapest and Lake Balaton, yet most tourists are in too much of a hurry to have a look. This is regrettable, for the old core of the town has been almost entirely liberated from motor traffic, giving visitors a green light for leisurely strolling and exploring.

Székesfehérvár claims to be the oldest of all Hungarian towns. In 1972 its thousandth anniversary was celebrated with the installation on a hilltop of a millenial monument resembling from afar a gigantic TV aerial of the "rabbit's ears" variety. By coincidence, one of the biggest local

Héviz thermal baths.

industries is the manufacture of television sets and radios.

According to tradition, the very first great Magyar prince, Árpád himself, set up camp at or very near Székesfehérvár's present location and claimed the territory for his tribe. The town itself is said to have been founded by the 10th century Prince Géza, whose son, Stephen I, made it the national capital.

Just a few steps east of the town's main square, you can't —and certainly shouldn't— miss the **Garden of Ruins** *(Romkert),* site of many a historic event. This sunken terrain of archaeological excitements, bigger than a football field, is nicely surrounded by grass. And around the walls of the Roman-style arcade protecting three of the garden's four sides are sculptural relics of the highest quality—though mostly reduced to fragments. Below, the foundations of the 11th-century basilica and coronation church may be seen. This is where the kings of Hungary, perhaps beginning with Stephen I, were crowned over five centuries. And here were buried most of the kings of the Árpád dynasty. Many monarchs expanded and modified the church from its original Romanesque simplicity. After the Turkish armies captured the town in the middle of the 16th century, the basilica was converted to a mosque. In 1601, when the Turks were besieged, the gunpowder they had stored in or around the building exploded, for reasons subject to dispute. It took archaeological teams more than a century to piece together all the remains of the devastated royal sanctuary.

The over-all annihilation of Székesfehérvár during and immediately after the Turkish era allowed the town to rebuild from the ground up. Some stylish Baroque buildings constructed in the 18th century provide the special atmosphere of central Székesfehérvár today.

Facing Szabadság tér, the main square of the old town, the most portentous building is the **Bishop's Palace** (*Püspöki palota*—at No. 10), built between 1790 and 1801. Medieval manuscripts and rare books are among 40,000 items in the palace library. On the south side of the square, the City Hall links two old palaces, one of two storeys, the other of three.

Another historic square, István tér, has an equestrian statue of St. Stephen himself in the middle. The neo-Classical County Hall is a 19th-century addition to the generally Baroque character of this scene. Around the corner, the old Carmelite Church contains outstanding Baroque frescoes, paintings and woodcarvings.

Heading west from Székesfehérvár on Route 8, the first town of consequence is **Veszprém,** a county seat with nearly 200 historic monuments. The most interesting part of this hill town is the **Castle District,** on a bluff that finally reveals a stirring panorama of Veszprém and its countryside—the Bakony mountains.

Heroes' Gate (*Hősök kapuja*) leads from the more lively part of town up to the castle area. Stones from the original medieval castle gate were used for this modern reconstruction. The zone beyond the gate is so narrow that there is room for only one street, Tolbuhin út (named after the World War II Soviet marshal). Of all the historic buildings, in various styles and colours, lining Tolbuhin út, the most significant may be the two-storey **Episcopal Palace.** It was completed in 1776, using the stones from the original royal palace that had stood on the site since the age of King Stephen. The Bishop of Veszprém traditionally crowned the queens of Hungary.

Next to the Bishop's Palace is the Gizella Chapel, with its 13th-century frescoes restored.

Further up the hill, the two-towered **Cathedral,** dedicated to St. Michael, has a history going back nearly a thousand years. Very few vestiges of the original church remain. Over the centuries

a series of disasters—the Mongol invasion, the Turkish siege, an Austrian assault, plus several apparently accidental fires—gave architects and reconstruction crews many opportunities to try new ideas. After going through Romanesque, Gothic and Baroque phases, the church was finally reconstructed at the beginning of the 20th century in neo-Romanesque style. Several of the altars and side-chapels are considered valuable works of art.

Veszprém is encircled by a ring road designed to keep out the through traffic—quite a rarity in Hungary. But it's well worth following the signs into Veszprém for a look at the Castle District as well as the vast housing projects in the flourishing centre of the new town.

If you have gone as far as Veszprém it's a 15-kilometre side-trip on Route 8 to the small industrial town of **Herend.** The porcelain produced at Herend has been known and prized in distant countries since the first half of the 19th century. The modern factory, faced with tile, is closed to the public, but a **museum** next door exhibits some of the classic products that built the Herend tradition.

Connoisseurs of medieval castles are accustomed to looking for them on dominating hilltops. But in the small village of **Nagy-vázsony,** 23 kilometres south-west

of Veszprém, the local **castle** stands *below* the rest of the town—no doubt for sound 15th-century reasons. It's a small, cosy castle, interesting enough to put Nagyvázsony firmly on the tourist map.

The central character in the story of this fortress is Pál Kinizsi, a robust miller's apprentice who became a Hungarian general. His military exploits so impressed King Matthias Corvinus that the king gave him the castle. A few years later, in 1479, General Kinizsi celebrated victory over a unit of the Ottoman empire by doing a triumphal dance (the story goes) while carrying a Turk in each hand and one between his teeth. The cover of Kinizsi's marble sarcophagus may be seen in the castle's chapel.

After crossing the moat, you climb the original stone spiral staircase up to the main hall of the keep, furnished with armour and a banquet table with a capacity of 14 diners. Two floors up is a small museum of local medieval relics and a model of the castle as it looked in its prime. Above that, an observation deck offers a sentry's view of the town and some uncommonly pretty country to the north and west. In the 18th century the castle was used as a prison. In a small tribute to this era, the ground floor of the keep serves as a gallery of instruments of torture; notice the stocks

113

for six miscreants seated side by side.

Just up the hill from the castle a small **Postal Museum** displays antique telegraph and telephone equipment, seals and stamps, and harnesses from postal coaches.

Approaching **Sümeg,** 22 kilometres north of Balatonederics on Route 84, you catch sight of a hilltop **fortress** as exciting as any castle in Spain—as if the little limestone mountain had been put there just to have the fort plopped on top like a bird in a nest.

It's a slog up around the hill to the castle entrance almost 900 feet high; they don't make it easy but you don't have to be a mountain-climber, either.

The citadel itself was built in the late 13th century, its insurmountable wall system in the 15th and 16th centuries. It will come as little surprise that this eyrie successfully resisted the attentions of the Turkish army which had been overrunning everything else in sight. But after a disastrous fire in 1713 the castle fell into disrepair, and it wasn't restored until the 1960s.

Below, in the town of Sümeg—which the Turks wiped out when they couldn't attain the castle—there are two 18th-century buildings of importance. Just at the bottom of the hill, the former Episcopal Palace (now a student hostel) is a Baroque complex neatly integrated into the terrain. And the **Parish Church** at Deák Ferenc utca 14, is remarkable for the quality and quantity of the murals inside, covering walls, ceiling and dome. Painted by Franz Maulbertsch—a labour of a year and a half—these are considered the finest Baroque frescoes anywhere in Hungary.

Héviz, a small town only 6 kilometres from the western end of Lake Balaton, has a lake of its own... but what a lake! With an area of nearly 11 acres, it is Europe's largest warm-water lake. The surface temperature almost never falls below 30 °C (86 °F), even in midwinter. In summer it feels like tepid bathwater; lilies thrive along the shore, as do oodles of baby fish. Health-seekers crowding the grass around the lake between dips make it look like a therapeutic Blackpool or Coney Island.

The mineral water of Lake Héviz, spewing from a crater in the bottom at a rate of some 23 million gallons per day, is said to be healthfully radioactive. Some patients are prescribed a daily ration of water to drink, but most loll about in it, either in the lake or in nearby hotels and public health institutions with pools. At the Hotel Thermal, foreign visitors can recover from the rigours of healthy living by sidling up to the gambling tables at the casino in the evening.

SOUTHERN HUNGARY

The sunny southernmost region of Hungary, down along the Yugoslav border, enjoys a favoured mixture of terrain and towns: mineral-rich hills, sun-coaxed vineyards, and a momentous share of historical sites. Culture and folk customs are kept alive here; so is the wildlife.

Pécs (rhymes with Aitch) is the industrial and cultural capital of the region, with a population above 170,000. From street to street its character changes suddenly: medieval, Turkish, Baroque, early 20th century, and vast new housing and shopping developments in bigger-than-life socialist style. The cultural collisions that created Pécs couldn't be more succinctly illustrated than in the main square, Széchenyi tér. A Turkish mosque stands at one end of the long, canted plaza, a Catholic church at the opposite end. On the mosque's dome a cross surmounts a crescent with ambiguous symbolism.

Pécs made its mark in the world long before the Turkish era. Settled by the Celts, it became an administrative centre of the Roman empire under the name of Sopianae. Later it was called Quinque Basilicas, a reference to its five churches. Hungary's first university was founded in Pécs in 1367, its first semi-public library less than a century later.

The Ottoman empire's designs on Pécs went unfulfilled for 17 years of on-and-off siege. At last, in 1543, the city surrendered, and Turkish commerce and culture, including literary activity, were superimposed on the Hungarian way of life. The main mosque, now the parish church at the top of Széchenyi tér, was built in honour of Pasha Kasim, "the Conqueror" (who later ruled Buda). The Turks were finally ousted in 1686.

Pasha Kasim's Mosque, of stone and brick, had a graceful minaret alongside, but this was demolished in the 18th or 19th century. In the 20th century many of the building's forgotten details were found and restored. Thus, some of the original calligraphy can be seen on the interior walls. A crucifix now stands over a Muslim prayer niche. The congregation is Hungarian and Catholic, but the great dome, the dim, diffused light, and the striped arches are from another world, and another age.

Just behind the mosque, the **archaeological collection** of the Janus Pannonius Museum fills seven rooms with enlightening displays on local prehistory and early history. One rare convenience here is that explanatory signs are printed in English and German as well as Hungarian.

The Janus Pannonius after whom this place, and several others, are named was a 15th-century bishop of Pécs, a philanthropist, poet and scientist.

In Janus Pannonius utca, a **museum** is devoted to the painter Tivadar Csontváry Kosztka (1853–1919), known in some circles as the Douanier Rousseau of the Danube. His huge peopled canvases in unexpected colours are augmented by modern Hungarian paintings and sculpture.

The **decorative arts collection** of the Janus Pannonius Museum occupies the oldest house in Pécs, one street north in Káptalan utca. The core of the house was rebuilt in Renaissance style in the 16th century; a Baroque wing was added a couple of hundred years later. Aside from the building itself you'll want to see the exhibition of ceramics within. Most of the 9,000 or so items here come from the Zsolnay porcelain factory, founded in Pécs in 1870 and still producing works of unique shapes and colours.

Across the street, the birthplace of the 20th-century artist Victor Vasarely is now a **museum** of his works. Vasarely was doing op art before most op art practitioners were born; here his creations, reverently displayed, are a must for any art lover. The voluminous cellars below the house are occupied by a geological museum.

The **Cathedral** *(Székesegyház)* of Pécs stands at the top of Dóm tér, a grand tilting square of stone relieved by trees and flowers. Each of the four corners of the building is topped by a tower. The oldest parts of the cathedral date from the 11th century, when the name "Pécs" was first used, but mostly it is a 19th-century reworking of Romanesque ideas. Hence the eleven arches of the main (south) façade in what is described as Tuscan Romanesque style. Inside, the cathedral seems even bigger. The flat ceiling, 72 feet high, is divided into compartments of various shapes and sizes for saintly paintings. Most of the wall space is occupied by Hungarian abstractions. Stairways on each side of the main altar lead down to the 11th-century crypt, which has five naves. Much of the original medieval stone sculpture is now displayed in a lapidarium to the east of the cathedral, built after the fashion of a Roman house.

Note on the colonnaded Cathedral façade the superb statues of the 12 apostles by Mihaly Bartalits.

More authentic Roman era vestiges have been found all around **Dóm tér,** which was the centre of an extensive 4th-century cemetery. Archaeologists were thrilled to uncover painted Paleochristian burial vaults, thought to be the only ones of that type in

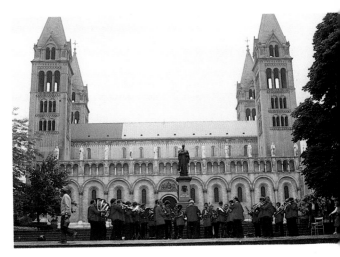

Pécs Cathedral.

central Europe. They belonged to the big landowners and the most highly esteemed local citizens.

West of the cathedral, at the corner of Esze Tamás utca and Landler Jenő utca, the medieval city walls come to life. The **Barbakán** (barbican), a circular, crenellated bastion, was put up at the entrance to the town in anticipation of assaults by the Turkish army. It was restored in the 1960s. As a gesture to peace, and 20th-century military tactics, a pleasant park now fills the moat.

The reinforced walls failed, of course, to turn back the Turks on their fourth try. One of the buildings recalling that era is a mosque in Rákóczi út, opposite the renovated Hotel Palatinus. The **Mosque of Pasha Hassan Yakovali** is the only one in Hungary with its minaret surviving. A small museum of Turkish armour, utensils and pottery is maintained inside the building.

Another 16th-century monument—in the western outskirts of Pécs—is the Mausoleum *(türbe)* of Idris Baba, at No. 8 Nyár utca. Many alterations affected the funeral chapel after the expulsion of the Turks; it was used as an ammunition dump in the 18th and 19th centuries, and the actual remains of Idris Baba were not discovered until 1961.

119

The **Mecsek Hills,** which rise from Pécs, provide fresh-air recreational possibilities. The wealth within the hills explains why Pécs is Hungary's fastest-growing city. Uranium mining began just west of the city in 1954; since then the population has almost doubled. But the boom town hasn't abandoned its centuries of cultural pretensions. It supports a symphony orchestra, a repertory theatre, an opera ensemble, and a ballet company that has won international acclaim for modern dance achievements.

Harkány, 26 kilometres south of Pécs, first came to notice in 1823. A labourer whose job kept him standing in a local swamp became aware of miraculous relief from his rheumatic ills. The first spa hotel was opened two years later. Now hotels, sanatoria, a camp site, a motel and other facilities make up an enormous resort complex in the middle of nowhere. The water, strong on sulphides, comes out of the earth at a temperature of about 62°C.

Siklós, a few miles east of Harkány, makes a cheerful excursion. The village has a major castle, very well preserved, with a history going back seven centuries. The **fortress** now houses a hotel with working wine-cellar, a restaurant, and a museum of local history (including some fearsome penal instruments from the Middle Ages). Also within the walls is a small **Gothic chapel** from the beginning of the 15th century, greatly admired for its frescoes and unusual ceiling stonework. The Siklós castle has been continually inhabited since its construction, a record that includes 143 years of Turkish occupation. As castles go, it's roomy and comfortable. And a princely view is enjoyed on all sides, for the castle stands atop its very own hill.

Mohács, on a lazy stretch of the Danube, is a resilient town, sunny but forever stigmatized with defeat. With the battle of Mohács—the infamous date was August 29, 1526—began 150 years of Turkish rule over Hungary. The field where King Louis II and his armies were wiped out by the Ottoman expeditionary force is now the site of a melancholy **memorial park** *(Mohácsi Történelmi Emlékhely).* Outstanding wood sculptures symbolizing the troops and generals of the opposing armies, the dead soldiers and the dying horses are spread across a battlefield-sized park. This moving monument to tragic combat was opened in 1976 on the 450th anniversary of the event. (To get to the park head south for 5 kilometres from the centre of Mohács, then turn west at the Sátorhelhi sign. The site is 2 kilometres farther on the left, the

Figure from Mohács Memorial Park.

120

Kalocsa is particularly renowned for its folklore.

entrance through a heroic iron grill gate.)

There are other memorials to the battle in the town itself, most notably the modern **Votive Church** in Széchenyi tér. It takes a Turkish form, though with a cross emphatically placed atop the dome.

Mohács is one of Hungary's biggest river ports, though no match for Budapest in its commercial prowess. Along the Danube here, watch the parade of cargo ships, ferries, fishing boats and pleasure craft go by. (If you're in Mohács at Carnival time, you can see a bizarre parade through the town, a Mardi Gras procession of revellers in the most colourful, scary costumes, welcoming spring and celebrating the expulsion of the Turks.)

The southernmost bridge across the Danube in Hungary—indeed, one of the very few Danube bridges south of Budapest—leads to the port town of **Baja.** The all-purpose single-lane bridge is used alternately by eastbound and westbound road traffic and by the railway as well—making it an extremely crucial crossing. Until the coming of the railway, Baja tugboat-men prospered in the trade with the Balkans.

Some of the old importance of the town may be sensed in the main square of Baja, Béke tér. It is about four times as big as local dignity could realistically require. The town hall has a balcony from which any orator would feel privileged to address the multitudes below. Similarly historic buildings line three sides of the square; the fourth extremity is a strip of garden overlooking the local river, a peaceful offshoot of the Danube. A beach and camping site enlivens the scene across the river on Petőfi island.

The **Forest of Gemenc** (*Gemenci-erdő*) occupies the west bank of the Danube, and a bit of the east shore as well, up- and downstream from Baja. This government-protected nature reserve, a stretch of forested moorland about 20 miles long and three to four miles wide, is alive with deer, wild boar and birds, big and small. It is a most restful place, except for the din of some of the world's noisiest frogs. There are two principal ways for tourists to see this national park: boat tours and a minitrain excursion. Aside from the natural attractions, the intricate locks of the modern Sió canal are worth a close look.

Back in Transdanubian wine-growing country, the businesslike town of **Szekszárd** remembers King Béla I. In 1061 he founded a Benedictine monastery here on what is now called I. Béla Square. The hilltop site of that fortified monastery is today occupied by the 19th-century County Hall, a classically-columned white palace with archaeological surprises in the courtyard—vestiges of the ancient abbey church and an even older chapel. In the centre of town, a dramatic aluminium sculptural ensemble enlivens the fountain in a small park alongside the municipal theatre.

If Hungary were to proclaim a folklore capital, it would most likely be **Kalocsa,** a farming town 6 kilometres east of the Danube. When it was founded in the 11th century, Kalocsa was on the river, but the watercourse later shifted, leaving the town high and dry. The marshy meadows that remain have turned out to be ideal for wheat, fruit and vegetables... and especially that most Hungarian crop, paprika peppers.

Even if you think you've seen everything, Kalocsa has something indisputably unique: the world's only **Paprika Museum** (across Marx tér from the open-air vegetable market). The Hungarians, who grow 40 per cent of all the paprika in the world, give credit to Mexico for "inventing" hot peppers. This small museum illustrates the evolution of paprika farming and processing, providing the last word on the science and romance of papri-culture.

A more conventional museum, the **Károly Viski Museum** in István út, deals with Kalocsa particularities in other fields. A series of rooms simulate the typical life of yore with old Kalocsa furnishings and decorations. In the comprehensive collection of costumes, even the black formal dresses look colourful. And there is a powerful exhibition of historic photographs of life in old Kalocsa.

Newest of the museums in this town that has more than its fair share of museums is the **Nicholas Schöffer Memorial House.** The artist, who now lives and works in Paris, was born here. His art, right in the forefront of modern ideas and conceptions, provides a strange contrast with the folkloric and traditional image associated with Kalocsa, and yet... somehow it all seems perfectly fitting and the evolution logical. In Schöffer's art, there are traces of Kalocsa.

István út, named after King Stephen, is a tree-lined avenue leading to the historic centre of town, Szabadság tér. A church has stood in this square since the 11th century. The present Baroque **Cathedral**, built in the 18th century, is the fourth church in the line. During restoration work in 1910 a tomb from the year 1203 was discovered in the crypt.

Across the square, the three-storey **Archbishop's Palace** manages to look stately in spite of the bilious colour of the paint chosen to decorate its Baroque façade. The 18th-century architect was a monk. The palace **library** is celebrated for its decorations as well as its books: a bible signed by Martin Luther, a bible written in Singhalese on palm-leaf, and more than 100,000 other volumes.

But tourists usually come to Kalocsa for the folklore. For a cross-section of local arts and handicrafts, look for the group of peasant-style houses in Tompa Mihály utca, one street west of the main highway. The **Kalocsa Folk Art Cooperative** *(Kalocsai Népművészeti Szövetkezet)* runs a small museum of antique furniture, farm implements and art works, as well as a gift shop. Here, too, you can see the flower-embellished embroidery and pottery for which Kalocsa is famous. On occasion, groups of local boys and girls in beautifully hand-embroidered costumes dance for the tourists. The poise of the youngsters, the vitality of the music and the brilliance of the costumes make a memorable introduction to the wide open spaces of Hungary east of the Danube.

GREAT PLAIN AND PUSZTA

More than half the territory of all Hungary consists of the Great Plain. Once it was prairie, puszta and swamp. Now the flatlands are mostly given over to orchards or vineyards or pasture or rippling fields of wheat. Or chemical factories or textile plants on the edges of towns of character, mercifully close to the plain's peace and quiet. All that's missing is a man-sized hill.

Kecskemét, 85 kilometres south-east of Budapest, is a typical Great Plains farm town grown into a well-rounded provincial city of nearly 100,000 population. It has a sizable wine industry, and a cannery, and factories producing machine tools, tape recorders,

knitwear and shoes. But Kecskemét is famous for its most traditional agricultural crop, grown in the biggest orchards of Hungary: juicy apricots.

Coachloads of tourists are marched into the **Town Hall** *(Városháza)*, built at the turn of the 20th century in what might be called a heavily embellished Hungarianized Secessionist style. Upstairs, in the ceremonial hall covered with patriotic frescoes, the visitors are treated to miniature bottles of the local pride: genuine Kecskemét apricot brandy. Then they are lectured about the town's history and achievements.

The Town Hall shares the main square, Kossuth tér, with three churches. In chronological order, they are a Franciscan church begun in the 15th century, a Protes-

tant church mostly built in the 17th century, and a Catholic parish church constructed between 1774 and 1806. In the garden in front of the Town Hall is a unique monument: a big block of stone split in two. The inscription reads: "Here one of Kecskemét's greatest sons broke his heart." At this spot the young playwright József Katona died of a heart attack in 1830. Another honoured local figure is the musicologist, composer and educator Zoltán Kodály (1882–1967), after whom a music-teaching institute in Kecskemét is named.

Beyond the main square three other more or less contiguous squares make up a central pedestrian precinct. In Szabadság tér, the former synagogue—a Moorish-style structure of the 19th century—now fulfills a temporal assignment as the House of Technology. On the opposite corner, note the once-daring Art Nouveau building, the Cifra Palace.

Typical Great Plains scenery, once outside the towns, is a no-man's land occasionally interrupted by a fenced-in compound embraced by the only trees within miles. The cottages have white walls and red roofs, and a typical wooden counterpoise leans over the well. A pig or a horse wanders about the garden.

One relic of regional life you're unlikely to see in the countryside is a windmill; they're almost all gone now. But a whitewashed old mill has been transplanted to the small town of **Kiskunfélegyháza,** south-east of Kecskemét. It stands in the courtyard of the one-time prison, now part of the local **museum** (at No. 9 Vörös Hadsereg útja, the main north-south highway). This museum contains one of those gory exhibitions of prison torture devices from past centuries. But on a positive note, you can see musical instruments and other complex handicraft projects built by prisoners of scrap materials in their spare time. (Incidentally, the *kun* in Kiskunfélegyháza and other regional names refers to the Cumanians, nomads who occupied this area in the 13th century.)

One unusually grand building in the centre of Kiskunfélegyháza is the Town Hall, completed in 1912, in frilly Hungarian style. With shops on the ground floor and offices and an exotic tower above, it's quite an eye-opener in this mostly rustic setting.

In the **Kiskunság National Park** *(Kiskunsági Nemzeti Park),* Hungary preserves more than 100 square miles of a landscape of startling contrasts: salt marshes and dense medieval forests, sand dunes and pastures. And memories of a way of life that has inspired poets and painters. Rare wildfowl nest in the tiny salt lakes

Gyula Castle.

here, and fashionable breeds of horses, cattle and sheep thrive on the grasslands. The biggest and best-known of the six separate areas comprising the national park is the **Bugac-puszta,** now a top tourist attraction.

Excursions to this moody prairie leave from Kecskemét and Kiskunfélegyháza. From the *csárda,* or wayside inn, of Bugac, tourists are driven in old-fash- ioned horse-carriages on a dirt track through the woods to the stable area. Hungarian cowboys in baggy white trousers and shirts and red waistcoats show the visitors the stables and corrals first. Then they put on a horse-show which combines aspects of a rodeo, a circus and a stagecoach competition. Prudent photographers save some film for the finale—the runpast of "wild"

horses, an enchanting spectacle of grace and freedom.

A less dynamic point of interest here is the Shepherd Museum, with exhibitions of pastoral costumes and relics of the puszta way of life.

South-west of the national park zone, the small town of **Kiskunhalas** used to have scores of windmills; only one is left (in Kölcsey utca). The town's fame

rests on the fine needlework of its lacemakers. The tradition of Halas lace was conceived at the beginning of the 20th century when the town's art teacher and a local needlewoman devised delicate new stitches for lacemaking. The cottage industry won wide acclaim. In the Lace House *(Csipkeház)*, at the town's main intersection (Kossuth Lajos utca and Route 53), you can spy on the needleworkers of today, sewing away more or less oblivious to visitors. A one-room museum contains a cross-section of their handiwork.

About halfway between Kecskemét and Szeged, near Kistelek, is the **Ópusztaszer National Memorial Park** *(Ópusztaszeri Nemzeti Történeti Emlékpark)*. This was the site of the historic conclave of seven tribal chieftains who founded the Hungarian state in A.D. 896. Archaeologists are hard at work here. On Constitution Day in August, thousands of Hungarians come to the spacious park to commemorate the first Magyars.

The Great Plain is bisected by an important river, the Tisza, which actually runs longer—inside Hungary—than its much better-known neighbour, the Danube. The usually easy-going, slowly winding Tisza is often wide enough to resemble a mini-Mississippi. Its unsavoury reputation for flooding has been improved

131

with the elimination of more than a hundred of its untidy zigs and zags and the construction of thousands of miles of levees.

Just over a century ago the city of **Szeged,** near Hungary's lowest-lying spot, took the full brunt of the angry, swollen Tisza. Szeged was almost completely swept away. After the deluge the centre of town was raised to a safer altitude, embankments were built, and boulevards and squares were laid out for Hungary's first planned city. Today the riverfront, once so menacing, is Szeged's most relaxed feature, with tree-shaded promenades, excursion boats, floating swimming pools as in the Seine in Paris. That sidewheeler moored near the main bridge, its funnels too tall to go under the bridge, is another permanent feature—a restaurant and nightclub.

When Hungarians think of Szeged (population more than 170,000), three local products usually spring to mind: the tasty Szeged salami, the highly-seasoned Szeged fisherman's soup, and the brightly decorated slippers manufactured here. These are as down-to-earth as any claims to fame, yet Szeged is a cultural centre as well. Because of its two universities, the atmosphere is uncommonly cheery and youthful.

The centre of town, **Széchenyi tér,** is more a city park than a conventional main square—some 12 acres of old trees, lawns, flower-gardens, fountains, monuments, and benches. The most prominent building here, the yellow City Hall, was redone in eclectic-Baroque style after the great flood. Each floor has its own style, shape and size and windows; shooting up from the middle of the building is an odd sort of clock tower, top-heavy with decorative details.

Leading south from here the main shopping street, Kárász utca, is a pedestrian area with a vengeance; cars on the busy cross-streets have to yield indefinitely to the leisurely flow of window-shoppers afoot.

Szeged's most monumental landmark, the **Votive Church** *(Fogadalmi templom),* is a neo-Romanesque marvel of the 20th century, with enough pinnacles and arches for a dozen ordinary churches. Its twin towers shoulder a total of eight clocks—all, amazingly, in time. The great façade of the cathedral, with mosaics of the apostles flanking a tall marble statue of the Virgin Mary, provides the backdrop for the Szeged Summer Festival of opera and ballet. The square, enclosed by matching arcades, is big enough to hold 6,000 seats; the acoustics are loudly praised. Inside the church there are frescoes of bright Hungarian patterns. The organ, at last report, was rated the 8th biggest in the world: some 11,000 pipes and 166 registers.

After the flood of 1879 the survivors vowed to build this memorial church. For 25 years they debated where to put it, so construction couldn't begin until 1913. Then they ordered the demolition of the remains of a 12th-century church standing in the way. But the medieval **Tower of St. Demetrius** refused to budge; dynamite didn't move it. So the tower, four-sided at the bottom and octagonal above, was finally left in peace, to add distinction to the new plaza.

Behind the cathedral, an 18th-century Serbian Church looks unprepossessing, but within are many worthy Orthodox icons. The Baroque iconostasis facing the congregation is sensational.

Roosevelt tér, the square named in honour of America's World War II president, is alongside the river at the central bridge. The terribly solemn building here, inscribed *A Közművelődésnek* above its Corinthian columns, is the Palace of Education and Culture. Don't let its title put you off, have a look inside: the **Ferenc Móra Museum** covers a lot of ground, from stuffed animals to Hun and Avar handicrafts to modern Magyar art. There are also reproductions of peasants' living quarters with authentic furniture and utensils.

The city plan of Szeged provided concentric ring roads to intersect the streets fanning out from the riverfront. The inner ring has been renamed Lenin körút. But the wide outer arc retains its original designations, with sections named after Rome, Berlin, Paris, London, Moscow and Vienna, cities which came to the aid of Szeged after the flood. Beyond Bécsi (Vienna) körút, in the district called Alsóváros (the Lower City), is a most significant monument. The former **Franciscan Church** in Mátyás király tér (King Matthias Square) was completed at the beginning of the 16th century in Gothic style. The elaborate Baroque furnishings inside the single-nave church came later—after the departure of the Turks. The lone tower, too, was an 18th-century afterthought.

Halfway between Szeged and the Romanian border crossing at Nagylak, the busy farmers' town of Makó is noted for its onions, a serious export crop for nearly a century. Though it bears no obvious resemblance to Baden-Baden, Makó is a spa town. Aside from the alkaline thermal baths, and fishing on the Maros river, there's not much excitement.

North-east of Szeged, where three rivers converge, the county of Békés is a favourite area for anglers, bathers and campers. In the county seat, **Békéscsaba**, one river branch pursues its sluggish course through the heart of town,

133

in the shade of weeping willows. Alongside is the **Mihály Munkácsy Museum** (at 9 Széchenyi út), dedicated to the 19th-century painter. On show are a few samples of his talent at portraiture and vignettes of Hungarian life. In the same building, archaeological and ethnological exhibits bring to life existence on the Great Plain. And in the building next door, a small museum contrasts the cultures of the Hungarians, Romanians, Czechs, Slovaks and Germans who settled in the district.

Gyula, just south-east of Békéscsaba, is known for its thermal baths, its vegetables, its spicy sausages, and its very old-fashioned Gothic **castle.** The brick fortress, windowless and all right-angles, was built at the end of the 14th century. Notwithstanding its fierce appearance and 10-foot-thick walls, the stronghold fell to the Turks in 1566. It was restored in the 1950s. Inside the former castle chapel, the local museum contains town documents and antiques, some extremely ancient.

Alongside the fort is a small lake chock-a-block with rowing boats, for hire by the hour. On the edge of the fortress park, Gyula's extended bathing area is built around medicinal springs; the alkaline water emerges at 70°C.

In many parts of rural Hungary, road signs warn of game at large, always indicated by the silhouette of a prancing deer. But on the way to Debrecen, the metropolis of the Great Plain, you may be startled to sight a pheasant thumping its wings across the highway just ahead of you. Or any number of smaller, less gawky birds. Wildlife is rife on the flatlands.

Debrecen, population nearly 200,000, is a centre of industry, a university town, and a historic bulwark of Protestantism in a mostly Catholic country. In 1540 the Reformation came to Debrecen. In 1552 only Protestants were allowed to settle in the city and the Catholic church was closed. The arrival of the Ottoman empire's armies three years later made these issues slightly abstract.

The long, straight main street of Debrecen, Vörös Hadsereg útja, runs almost head-on into the neo-Classic eminence of the **Great Church** *(Nagytemplom).* Like many historic buildings here, it is painted an off-yellow. A church has stood on this site since the 12th century, but the present Calvinist cathedral, with tall twin towers and a colonnaded façade, was designed in 1805. In the tower on the left hangs a five-ton bell—called the largest in Hungary—first cast by order of the ruling prince of Transylvania,

19th century architecture in the centre of Szeged.

György Rákóczi I, in 1636. (It had to be recast after a 19th-century fire.)

Compared to the many Baroque Catholic churches of Hungary, the stark white interior of the Great Church comes as a surprise. But the lack of ornamentation emphasizes the beauty of the Empire-style pulpit and the 3,000-pipe organ. This church, the biggest Protestant church in Hungary, was the scene of a dramatic secular happening. In April 1849 the Hungarian parliament, meeting inside the Great Church, voted to depose the House of Habsburg.

The building of the **Calvinist College** *(Református Kollégium)*, behind the Great Church, claims more recent historical attention. In December 1944, while most of Hungary was still under German

control, an anti-Nazi Provisional National Assembly was convened here, one month after the arrival of the Soviet army.

The **Déri Museum,** the easternmost of Hungary's major provincial museums, faces Múzeum utca at Déri tér. The ethnographic department is well endowed with magnificently decorated shepherds' coats from the nearby puszta area, and a wealth of folk art from the region. Archaeological items run from the finds of local digs to a couple of handsome Egyptian mummies. The oriental arts department can boast a smallish but beautifully chosen collection, mostly of porcelain and sculpture. But the museum is best known for its gallery of

Hortobágy puszta and figure in Shepherd Museum.

137

Hungarian art. A large, bright room is devoted to Mihály Munkácsy, whose paintings range from a depiction of a barroom brawl to a sweeping biblical documentary, *Ecce Homo*.

At the top end of the main street, diagonally across from the Great Church, the venerable **Arany Bika Hotel** exercises a large and beneficial presence. Arany Bika means Golden Bull; the hotel was founded in 1699. Have a look at the nostalgia-soaked main dining room with chandeliers descending from a stained-glass ceiling three storeys high.

On the main street itself, with its six traffic lanes and two pairs of tram tracks down the middle, a most unusual church stands at the corner of Széchenyi utca. This small Protestant church was built in Baroque style in the early 18th century, but a storm toppled its dome. Instead of replacing it with a similar bulbous steeple, they had the romantic idea of building a crenellated bastion tower.

North of the central business district of Debrecen, nicer residential areas lead to the Nagyerdő (Big Forest), a park of more than 5,600 acres interspersed with swimming pools and thermal baths, a zoo, and other recreational facilities.

But for a unique experience in the great outdoors, head west on Route 33 into the puszta. For a start, this is as pleasant a stretch of highway as you'll find anywhere in Hungary. Straight and comfortably wide, with the shade of two rows of trees for mile after mile, it pierces flat fertile farmland. And then it enters the **Hortobágy National Park,** where the timeless scenery of the mysterious puszta is preserved. The road unfolds like a causeway above the surface of an eerie sea, half land, half water. Marsh and farmland alternate, wild flowers and grassy swaths and alkaline wastelands, and an occasional clump of trees finds a foothold in the spongy soil. Birds as fascinating as the large white-fronted goose make this a compulsory stop on their migrations. You may also observe white and black storks, heron, falcon, even eagles.

Land of Illusion

Don't look now, but one of the most talked-about "sights" on the puszta is just a mirage.

Lucky visitors see amazing visions: cattle grazing at a non-existent pond, disembodied church steeples, phantom villages. It's all explained as the waves of hot air shimmering upward from the sun-baked earth, distorting perspective between the viewer and the flat horizon.

If you miss the mirage, or can't summon up a hallucination, stick around for the genuine puszta sunset—as romantic as anywhere on earth.

The main crossroads of the region is in the village of **Hortobágy** itself, near the charming **Nine-Arched Bridge.** The span was finished in 1833, to the surprise of all who thought Hungary's longest stone bridge would be an engineering fiasco. The herdsmen glamorized it as "the bridge built on nine holes". Long before the bridge was designed, an inn catered to travellers here. The **Nagycsárda,** reconstructed at the end of the 18th century and again in the 19th century, has guest rooms and a restaurant with a folkloric menu. Otherwise the village mainly consists of neat cottages for the farmers and modern official buildings.

A large, round, thatch-roofed building next to the main car-park is a **museum** explaining the Hortobágy National Park, Hungary's largest. Photos and charts cover the park's history and natural resources—including, at recent count, over 6,000 cattle, 600 horses, and 100,000 sheep. The museum posts all captions and notices in German, English and Russian as well as Hungarian—a handy idea for foreign tourists. The **Shepherd Museum** (*Pásztormúzeum*), in a whitewashed barn across the road, displays carriages, saddles and bells from olden times, musical instruments, and the costumes used by cowboys and herdsmen—from party gear to fur coats.

On the other side of the *csárda,* somebody had the happy idea of opening an art museum in the middle of the wilderness. The subject of all the paintings is the puszta: the haunting landscape, the shepherds and their animals.

Traditional fairs and horse-shows are still held at Hortobágy. Or you can tour a horse-breeding farm (2 kilometres north of the bridge), or ride in a carriage or on horseback. City folk in their riding boots sometimes draw stares from the locals, though the powerful but gentle horses take it all in stride. Horses of the Nónius breed have been raised here for more than a century.

On the edge of the puszta, 21 kilometres south-west of Debrecen, a spa town with the difficult name of **Hajdúszoboszló** calls itself "the Mecca of Rheumatics" for short. Surrounded by forest and pasture, this prosperous-looking town centres on a big health and leisure park including a sizeable boating lake. But the big attraction for hundreds of thousands of Hungarian and foreign visitors each year is the brownish mineral water. Discovered by oil prospectors in the 1920s, the spring now supplies a luxury hotel as well as health resorts run by various trade unions. A historic footnote in Hajdúszoboszló is a 20-yard segment of the 15th-century fortress wall and a restored round tower.

139

Street of the Baroque inner
city of Eger.

NORTHERN HIGHLANDS

Between the Great Plain and the
Czechoslovakian border, most of
Hungary's timberland is concentrated on a series of minor mountain ranges. Oak, beech and pine
grow thick over the hills and
valleys of this fresh-air zone of
nearly 4,000 square miles. This is
Hungary's winter sports region,
with ski-jumps, ski-runs and
sleigh-rides. Summer visitors
ramble among the waterfalls,
lakes and vineyards, and towns.

Of the five ranges of mountains
in the northern highlands the Mátra range is best supplied with
resorts, picnic grounds and look-
out points. Summiteers come here
to find the country's highest
point, the Kékestető peak (altitude 3,330 feet). If you need a
base camp for the Mátra, the
regional capital is the industrial
town of **Gyöngyös**. By way of
sightseeing, a couple of old
churches are pointed out: St. Bar-
tholemew's Church, in the main
square, considered Hungary's
largest Gothic church, dates from
the middle of the 14th century,
though much revised since then.
The former Franciscan church in
Nemecz József tér is old enough
to have been burned out in 1526

and restored in Baroque style nearly 200 years later.

But of all the highland towns the most compelling is surely Eger, endowed with wine, thermal waters, nearly 200 historic monuments, and a personality all its own.

Eger, population about 60,000, was one of the early Hungarian towns, with a bishop from the beginning of the 11th century. After the Mongol hordes annihilated Eger and most of its inhabitants in 1241, settlers from western Europe helped to repopulate and rebuild the town. But the indelible trauma for Eger was the Turkish era, a time of siege and slaughter, hope and despair.

In 1552—11 years after Buda had fallen to Islam—Eger's defenders turned back the Turkish army, sending a wave of relief to the furthest reaches of Christendom. It was the first defeat for the rampaging Turks, and a bad blow for their image of invincibility.

Alas, the sequel to the heroic defence of the Eger castle was a second siege 34 years later, and this time the Turks routed the garrison. Eger became a Turkish provincial capital; mosques and baths were built during nearly a century of Turkish occupation. The town was retaken by Hungary in 1687, only a year after the liberation of Buda.

You can explore the craftily designed casemates and bulwarks of the **fortress,** much restored but still heavy with memories. And even if history and military engineering are not your most urgent interests, the view from this hilltop is one of a kind—a skyline of Baroque towers setting off the long, thrusting turret of Europe's northernmost medieval minaret.

Memories of the heroes and heroines of the first (1552) siege are stressed in the exhibits, monuments and inscriptions in the fortress today. The **castle museum,** named in honour of Captain István Dobó, who commanded the defence, has an ample display of Hungarian and Turkish weapons and armour, coins and utensils.

In the centre of the inner city below, the main medieval market square is called Dobó István tér, with a plume-hatted statue of the castle commander himself, sword upraised. Also among the tulip beds of the square is another sculptural memorial to the siege —a bloodthirsty equestrian ensemble of Magyar versus Turk in close combat.

Facing Dobó István tér is the former **Minorite Church** (*Minoritak temploma*), painted pink and cream with green-topped towers. Beneath this unconventional colour scheme it's an attractive example of 18th-century Baroque architecture. The church was dedicated to St. Anthony of Padua, the subject of a number of frescoes and paintings inside, and a statue on the façade. Offsetting the harmonious design of the church is a modern department store erected on the opposite side of the square.

From Minorite to Minaret is only a short walk northward to Knézich Károly utca at Torony utca. The 14-sided **Kethuda minaret,** 130 feet tall, would be a gem on any skyline. The original stone parapet of the circular balcony, from which the muezzin would sound the call to prayer, has been replaced by an iron railing. The very top of the structure was restored in the 19th century. (Of course, a mosque originally stood beside the minaret, but it was demolished in 1841.)

Eger's 19th-century **Cathedral,** the second largest church in Hungary, looks like a windowless palace of justice imitating a Greek temple. But, inside, the atmosphere is light and bright, from windows in the dome. On either side of the ceremonial steps leading up to the basilica are heroic statues—of Hungarian royal saints Stephen and Ladislas and the apostles Peter and Paul. Other giant statues stand atop the façade. These, and most of the reliefs inside the church, are by a Venetian sculptor, Marco Casagrande (1804–80). The dome frescoes are of recent vintage.

Across the square from the cathedral, a sprawling 18th-century institution, originally the Lyceum or secondary school for girls, is now called the Ho Chi Minh Teachers' Training College *(Ho Si Minh Tanárképző Főiskola).* The biggest Baroque building of its kind in Hungary includes an astronomical observatory tower, with a museum on the top floor.

Otherwise, the centre of Eger is meant for strolling and discovering. Among the quaint touches are modern sculptures over the doors of shops, whimsically announcing the speciality of the house. One very important speciality is wine, for Eger is the home of the Hungarian wine most widely known abroad—*Egri bikavér,* meaning Bull's Blood of Eger. This robust red wine, as well as less famous local varieties, may be sampled in clearly marked wine taverns in the old town, or at traditional wine cellars where the vineyards meet the city.

Sixty kilometres north-east of Eger is Hungary's second biggest city, Miskolc, with heavy industry pouring forth sunset-coloured smoke. Between the two towns you can catch your breath in the **Bükk Mountains,** a sanctuary of waterfalls and dense forest. You may not spot the lumberjacks at work but you'll find fresh logs stacked beside the back roads.

The main street of **Miskolc,** Széchenyi utca, throbs with a steady traffic of trams, trucks and cars. Along the thoroughfare are a number of valued 18th- and 19th-century buildings, including the County Hall and the City Hall, facing each other.

Miskolc (population about 210,000) has its own mountain—a hill, really— just a short walk south of the main street. Among the curiosities of Avas Mountain *(Nagy-Avas)* are hundreds of man-made caves, many of them centuries old, used for storing wine. On the slopes of the hill facing the town stands a 13th-century Gothic church, known simply as the **Calvinist Church.** It was enlarged in the 14th and 15th centuries, plundered by the Turks in 1544, and rebuilt in the 1560s as a Protestant church. Alongside, a separate bell tower now equipped with an automatic carillon rises to a tall wooden-roofed spire. The churchyard, a jumble of monu-

ments of marble, stone and wood, has been used as a cemetery for nine centuries.

Many cities, in Hungary as much as elsewhere, feel the need for a status symbol such as a soaring TV tower with an observation deck or restaurant, or both, towards the top. Miskolc shrewdly put a café and lookout platform on Avas Mountain, and then built the TV tower on top of

that. On a good day you can see as far as the Carpathian Mountains.

Another place to go for a superior panorama is the recently restored **Diósgyőr Castle,** on the western hills of Miskolc. With its four square crenellated towers, this 13th-century fortress was a favourite home of the Angevin King Louis the Great. It is sometimes called the queen's castle, for it became part of the dowry of the queens of Hungary. The chapel was last used in 1776.

The most desirable suburb of Miskolc, **Lillafüred,** is linked to the city by a narrow-gauge railway (terminus at Esperanto Square) as well as a bus line. Set among forests, mountain streams and a waterfall, Lillafüred has many handsome villas and a grand old pre-war hotel, now a trade union resort, equipped with hanging gardens. Just up the hill is the entrance to the Limestone-Tufa Cave, with exotic stalactite formations. Excursion groups are given guided tours.

People who really know about caves become ecstatic about the **Aggtelek** region of forests, rolling farmland and karst outcroppings, north of Miskolc, up against the Czechoslovakian border. Here the **Baradla Cave** has been known for thousands of years; the remains of Stone Age spelunkers

Memorial to the siege of Eger on Dobó István tér.

145

have been found inside. The original cave (*barlang* is the Hungarian word) is 22 kilometres long, including a stretch under the frontier into Czechoslovakia, but substantial additions have been found.

Guided tours of about one hour (normally in Hungarian only) leave from the entrances at Aggtelek or Jósvafő. The standard route passes through one cavern after another, in which giant rock arches and dripstones are illuminated. Stalactites and stalagmites of the most fanciful designs are being created by the constant drip of moisture through the limestone. There are incipient stalactites like cobwebs on the ceiling, and colossal finished columns thousands of years old. In the biggest cavern, called the Concert Hall, a fountain plays, lighting effects are added, and a tape of a resonant Bach organ piece sounds off to demonstrate the acoustics. It's extremely damp underfoot and overhead; remember to take along a coat or sweater for the refreshing underground temperature—between 10° and 11°C (50° to 52°F).

The Tisza river, which last came to our attention when it flooded the southern city of Szeged, arrives in Hungary from the north-east. Among its many twists and turns is a 90-degree digression at the spot where the scenic Bodrog river joins it. This beautiful, crucial confluence is the site of Hungary's most famous little town: **Tokaj.**

At first glance, from afar, Tokaj and its small mountain looks too good to be true. Even if they did plant one of those boring TV towers on the summit, it's a joy to see the vineyards climbing higgledy-piggledy, some at a stately incline, others terraced, still others askew but hanging on. This, of course, is where the "wine of kings and king of wines" comes from. But it's not the only place, for 28 communities up and down the county combine forces in the Tokaj wine-growing region.

Tokay's renown from medieval times has produced a bumper crop of vintage anecdotes. Pope Benedict XIV, acknowledging a gift of Tokay from the Empress Maria Theresa, intoned: "Blessed be the land that yielded thee, blessed the lady who sent thee, and blessed be me for having tasted thee." Other ringing endorsements have been collected from the likes of Frederick the Great, Voltaire, Anatole France, Goethe, Heine, Schubert and Beethoven.

You will be impatient to discover the cause of such enthusiasm. The wine cellars of Tokaj are just the place. A generous glass of Tokay *ordinaire* costs perhaps twice the price of an ice-cream; the sweeter, stronger variants of the golden wine are dearer.

Otherwise, you might drop in on the local **wine museum.** In a former wine cellar, old methods of production are illustrated by, among other things, a huge 19th-century grape press. There is also a novel display of labels from foreign imitations of genuine Hungarian Tokay.

Finally, one more castle to round out the scene in north-east Hungary. Only 13 kilometres from the Czechoslovakian border, **Sárospatak Castle** is one of Hungary's great monuments, for its size, history and state of repair. And the setting, overlooking the wooded banks of the Bodrog river, makes this a stronghold of beauty.

The nucleus of the rambling fortifications is the **Red Tower** *(Vöröstorony),* a six-storey bastion built at the end of the 15th century. The Renaissance stone carvings and details which distinguish the castle came later, when craftsmen were imported from Italy to add grace to the utilitarian defences. Over the centuries additional buildings in succeeding architectural styles went up around the original keep. Guided tours cover the highspots, from the cellar fortifications to the top deck of the Red Tower, which is big enough to parade a platoon of troops. The views down and out through the cannon embrasures are spellbinding.

147

WHAT TO DO

Whether you prefer serious or light-hearted activities, Hungary can respond to most tastes. If your idea of a holiday is nothing more complicated than swimming, boating and wine-tasting, Lake Balaton might be your best choice. But if you're the type to potter about Roman ruins, try Budapest's Aquincum, or Székesfehérvár or Szombathely. Some single-minded tourists come to Hungary expressly for the birdwatching, or horseriding, or to sink into a therapeutic thermal bath.

Happily, it's easy to combine many activities in a country the size of Hungary. You can cover museums and sports, boat excursions and operas, profitable shopping and folklore spectacles. And still find time for the renowned food and drink.

Shopping

Handicrafts dominate the shopping list for most tourists. Hungary's artisans strive to devise new lines as well as meeting the demand for the dependable traditional designs. You may also want to browse through the low-priced books and records. Foodstuffs are another national speciality—suitable for export.

The price tag tells the whole story in Hungarian shops. A VAT or sales tax of 25%, included in the price, is added to most goods and services (see p. 168).

In addition to all the normal retail outlets, tourists can find a select range of Hungarian and imported goods in Intertourist and Utastourist shops (many of them in hotels), which accept hard currency only. Prices are usually listed in U.S. dollars, but almost all convertible currencies and credit cards are accepted.

149

Two special shops in Budapest sell art, antiques and coins for foreign currency only. Keep your receipts in case of any questions at customs—on leaving Hungary or returning home.

Hungary's Best Buys

Antiques. Paintings, furniture, vases, jewellery, coins, leather-bound books, knick-knacks. The items for sale in hard-currency shops are suitable for export; in other shops, be sure to ask whether it's permitted to take the goods out of Hungary. (Precious art works may not leave.)

Books. Hungarian publishers produce very inexpensive picture books, travel guides and literary works written in or translated into English, French, German, Italian and Spanish.

Carpets and rugs. Warm colours, rugged fabrics and harmonious designs distinguish Hungarian carpets and rugs of all sizes. They're advantageously priced—even the homespun, handknotted originals.

Ceramics. The best-known of the Hungarian factories, at Herend, near Lake Balaton, has been turning out porcelain plates, cups and vases since 1839. Other firms operate at Kalocsa and Pécs. Most of the designs available may be floral, but you'll even see imitation Chinese vases. Porcelain figurines of typical Hungarian characters are also popular.

Copper and brass. Plates, bowls, vases, ashtrays—and Turkish-style coffee sets.

Elixir. Some foreigners fly to Hungary just to buy bottles of the much-publicized tonic and suspected cure-all called Béres Csepp. Sold only at shops of the Herbaria enterprise; no prescription necessary.

Food products. Some items can be hand-carried out of the country: paprika in sachets or the ready-made sauce in tubes; strudel or cakes packed in sturdy boxes by the better confectioners' shops; and salami—the highest-quality Hungarian spicy sausage, full-size or in more portable dimensions. (For export restrictions, see p. 167–8.)

Furs. Small private workshops transform Hungarian and imported pelts into stylish winter hats and coats at very competitive prices.

Hair lotion. Thinning hair is said to be arrested by the use of Bánfi capillary lotion, another of Hungary's alleged miracle cures from the Herbaria shops, and at ordinary perfumeries as well. (If it works, forget the fur hat.)

Kitsch. If you're in the mood, buy a model of a Portuguese caravel with "Budapest" inscribed on the sail, or a simple air thermometer enshrined in a Rococo setting worthy of a reliquary—also marked "Budapest" as an afterthought.

Leather goods. Cowboy's whip and matching winebottle… from the Hungarian puszta. If time permits, you can have a pair of shoes made to fit and to last. Other interesting buys include leather gloves and wallets.

Linens. Embroidered table-cloths, napkins, doilies; each region, and virtually every village, has its own traditional designs.

Liqueurs and wine. The local apricot, cherry or plum brandy makes an inexpensive souvenir. Or take home a bottle of the best Tokay wine (some types come in gift packs).

Records and tapes. Aside from Liszt and Bartók, works galore. Hungarian performers have recorded many classic and modern pieces; also folk music, gypsy violins, Hungarian pop—all at low prices.

Rubik's puzzles. Professor Ernő Rubik began by inventing his addictive Magic Cube to challenge your three-dimensional imagination. Then came the daunting Snake. What next from the resident genius of Budapest's Academy of Applied Arts? Check the shops.

Shirts and blouses. Embroidered in primary colours, peasant-style blouses are a long-lasting reminder of Hungary. Men's shirts, off the rack or made to measure, include some bargains.

Silver. The workmanship of trays, pitchers, candelabra and smaller items is highly regarded, and the prices are considered extremely favourable.

Woodwork. Look for peasant-carved boxes big and small, bowls, walking sticks and chess sets.

Sports

For spectators or participants, Hungary offers a busy little world of sports. The strongest points involve horses and ball games, but there's something for almost everyone. The only sportsmen likely to be disappointed are visiting scuba divers and deep-sea fishermen.

Soccer, known by its Magyar name, *labdarúgás* (literally, kick-ball), draws the largest crowds. The big matches take place in Budapest's Népstadion, or People's Stadium, with its graceful dimensions and full range of equipment. If you can't get a ticket, there are more than 3,200 other soccer grounds in the country.

Basketball, water-polo and athletics—fields in which Hungary often does well internationally—also attract sizeable audiences.

One of the pleasures of going to the races at the local tracks is looking at the spectators: workingmen, universal horse-players in Damon Runyon stripes and little old ladies who seem to be respected handicappers. Flat

151

races *(galopp)* are run Sundays and Thursdays in summer, trotting races, year-round on Wednesdays and Saturdays. (Off-track betting at state lottery offices is also legal.)

Active Sports

Hungarians have a thousand years' experience in breeding —and riding—horses, so this is a good place to go for a canter. You can ride for an hour, or sign up for a course of lessons, or join a week-long trek.

There are dozens of stables, riding schools and horse-farms throughout Hungary, near Budapest or Lake Balaton if you're staying put, or in the middle of the puszta, or wherever you'd like to ride. Package-tours for horse-lovers start at many points in the country. An illustrated brochure, *Riding in Hungary*, gives details of the tour arrangements and tells about the individual riding schools and stud farms. It's available from IBUSZ, Cooptourist and similar firms, or from a specialized agency, Pegazus Tours, at Károlyi Mihály u. 5, 1053 Budapest. At the end of your holiday, if you simply can't bear to part with your clever Hungarian horse, you may be able to buy it and take it home.

If you'd rather be saddled with a bicycle, a cycling tour is a good way to combine healthful exercise with sightseeing. IBUSZ does pedalling tours to sites within a 30-mile radius of Budapest, as well as excursions based at Balaton; they go on for a week or more.

On a hot summer's day, you may seek nothing more strenuous than a swim. Pools are found in most towns.

For sailing and board-sailing (windsurfing), the place to go is Lake Balaton or, closer to Budapest, Lake Velence. Fishing in the lakes or rivers requires a permit from the Hungarian National Fishing Association (MOHOSZ), Október 6. u. 20, Budapest V. At Lake Balaton, permits may also be obtained on the spot from the travel agencies Siótour or Balatontourist Nord.

Tennis is popular in Hungary but facilities for visitors are limited. Your best bet is one of the big modern hotels, especially along Lake Balaton. Visiting golfers can tee off at the Kisoroszi course, 38 kilometres north of Budapest—or make do with mini-golf, played mostly around Balaton.

Hunting excursions attract thousands of western tourists to Hungary in search of wild boar or fox (all year round) or, seasonally, stag, roebuck, fallow-deer, pheasant or waterfowl. Several operators specialize in hunting holidays and organize complete hunting "packages". Further information can be had through the tourist office.

Nature Up-close

Conservancy areas make up about five per cent of all the territory of Hungary. There are three major national parks, 28 nature reserves and more than 100 small reserves, plus hundreds of parks deemed of local rather than national significance.

The largest of the national parks, in the Hortobágy, preserves the grasslands, rushes and reeds and alkaline ponds of the puszta. Keep an eye out for the wild flowers, exotic sheep, and perhaps a stork swooping in as ponderously as a pterodactyl.

The Kiskunság National Park, even younger than the Hortobágy, also specializes in the scenery, zoology, history and legend of the puszta, scattered over six enclaves.

The Bükk National Park, in the northern highlands, protects the prettiest forests in Hungary, interspersed with waterfalls and caves.

In 1952 the first national nature conservation zone was proclaimed on the Tihany peninsula, extending into Lake Balaton. It's still unspoiled, even though the most heavily travelled tourist routes pass just alongside.

Hungary takes pride in its arboreta and botanical gardens. In Budapest the Municipal Botanical Gardens are attached to the zoo. On the outskirts of Szombathely, the Jeli Arboretum is noted for its conifers from Asia, North America and southern Europe. At Szarvas, on the Great Plain, more than a thousand species of trees and plants, some most rare, grow in an arboretum founded in the 18th century. In the Danube Bend, the Botanical Gardens at Vácrátót boast 23,000 different species of flowers, trees and plants.

Thermal Baths

Sometimes it seems half the population of Hungary has landed in hot water. And the ones who aren't soaking in the thermal baths are drinking the mineral water. It's been the national pastime since the days of the Romans. The statistics: about 500 hot springs in Hungary gush forth more than 130,000,000 gallons of health-giving water every day.

Hungarian spas don't have names as easy to remember as Spa (the watering-place near Liège, Belgium, very chic in the 19th century). But by Magyar standards some are extremely terse: Balf, Gyula, Hévíz... though not Hajdúszoboszló. Best of all are the spas combining health, comfortable accommodation, scenic or historic significance and recreational possibilities. Here are a few that stand out, their specialities indicated by the abbreviations L for locomotor disorders, G for gynaecological complaints,

I for intestinal problems and D for dermatological treatment.

In Budapest:

Császár Baths, a thousand years old; 16th-century Turks built the thermal pool. Twelve springs converge here. L.

Gellért Baths. Under the same roof as the old aristocratic hotel; a favourite of gout sufferers. LG.

Hotel Thermal, Margaret Island. Halfway between Buda and Pest, everything from mud packs to dentistry. LG.

Rudas Baths. Another real Turkish bath; of the 15 springs feeding this bath, Juventus is the best known of its drinkable mineral waters. LI.

Széchenyi Baths. This one is in Pest, in the middle of City Park; one of Europe's largest. LGI.

In the provinces:

Balatonfüred. Carbon dioxide springs and the Lake Balaton climate are said to help heart and circulatory ailments. L.

Balf is close enough to the Austrian border to have developed a significant clientèle of foreigners. LGID.

Bükfürdő. Even closer to Vienna. LI.

Gyula. Within sight of a medieval fortress, three springs provide water with a high iodine-bromine content. LI.

Hajdúszoboszló. Modern facilities on the edge of the puszta offer underwater massage, sauna, electrotherapy. LGD.

Harkány. Hungary's southernmost spa boasts an almost Mediterranean climate and sulphuric waters. GI.

Hévíz. Just west of Lake Balaton, this hot-water lake and its radioactive mud attract Hungarian and international patients. L.

Detailed information on Hungary's leading spas, their medical particulars and accommodation, are contained in a brochure, *Thermal Baths in Hungary,* available from travel agencies.

Entertainment

The entertainment calendar is crammed in Budapest and often promising in the provinces. All the wholesome attractions you'd expect are heavily subsidized—opera at its grandest, classical and contemporary drama, symphonies and chamber music, and keenly tuned folklore. While the emphasis is on cultural uplift, a few hedonistic surprises sneak in as well.

The schedules of operas, concerts, folklore performances and other attractions of interest to foreign tourists are published in *Programme in Hungary,* issued free every month with parallel texts in German, English and French. It also lists major jazz and pop concerts, as well as rock concerts approved for young people.

Theatre

Theatrical life is extremely active: on average, several new productions are given premières in Hungary each week. Though the language poses a problem where drama is concerned, there's no obstacle to sharing the wealth of the musical scene.

Musical Life

Opera, operetta, concerts, ballet and recitals follow a year-round rhythm. When the opera houses and concert halls close for the summer, outdoor venues take over: spectacular opera productions under the stars on Budapest's Margaret Island or before authentic ancient backdrops, and concerts and recitals in castle courtyards or monastery gardens. The performances are impeccable by any standards, and the costumes and sets resplendent, yet tickets remain relatively affordable compared with the prices in many Western capitals.

Festivals

To quicken the pace of cultural life, there are annual festivals and special events. The Budapest Spring Festival in March shows off the best in Hungarian music, dancing and art. In late September and October, Budapest Art Weeks provide the framework for special international concerts and theatrical programmes.

155

Among the regional festivals in distinctive settings: the Szeged Festival (July-August), with opera and drama performed before the vast Votive Church; Martonvásár Beethoven Concerts (June) in the former castle of the Brunswick family 32 kilometres southwest of Budapest where Beethoven is thought to have composed his *Moonlight Sonata*; Sopron Festival Weeks (June) in the medieval atmosphere of the inner town; Fertőrákos cave concerts (June-July) in the ancient quarry; and the Gyula Castle Plays (July) in the 14th-century fortress.

Folklore

Folklore performances, amateur and professional, take place frequently not only at festivals but in theatres all year round. You may see a dance troupe from a local factory, or an internationally recognized professional folk-dance company. In Budapest a folklore show is scheduled most nights at the Municipal Folklore Centre, Fehérvári út 47 (southern Buda).

The dancers, wearing brilliant costumes, are full of spirit and enthusiasm—just like the music. They can even sing while they whirl and stomp their boots. The accompaniment may be provided by a large orchestra including a cymbalom, an instrument related to the dulcimer with a tone resembling at times a banjo, harp or harpsichord; it's a thrill to hear when a master performs at hair-raising speed. The repertoire runs from the *csárdás* to boot-slapping Lads' Dances, wedding dances and dances devised in the 18th century to lure country bumpkins to army recruiting officers.

Films

Hungarians are keen film-goers. But the tourist is out of luck, because most foreign movies are dubbed into Hungarian.

Nightlife

Turning to the racier side of Budapest nightlife, establishments with names as exotic as the Moulin Rouge and Maxim's present international floor-shows with big production numbers, including glamorous, minimally dressed dancers. But strip-tease is ruled out. The nightclubs open at 10 p.m. and keep going, noisily and expensively, until 4 or 5 a.m. Elsewhere in town, mostly in and near the major hotels, are nightspots with dancing but no show. You'll also notice scores of discotheques and inviting, dimly-lit bars; both keep late hours.

For visitors who prefer the excitements of the gambling casino, the Budapest Hilton provides roulette, baccarat, blackjack and slot machines in a discreet atmosphere, while the Lido offers roulette and slot machines. All transactions are in deutsche marks, and most of the conversation is in German, except for the obligatory *"Faites vos jeux, messieurs"*.

DINING

When it comes to dining out, Hungarians don't miss a chance to reaffirm the joy of living. Even a modest restaurant posts a 20- or 30-item menu every day, and the food is as good as it is abundant. The wines maintain a 2,000-year record of excellence. As likely as not, music accompanies the festivities—gypsy violins or some provincial group interpreting songs from ancient hit-parades. The waiters are efficient and attentive. And when it's time for the bill, there's no need for foreboding. By the standards of western Europe, it's all a bargain.

Because paprika has been associated with Hungarian cooking for several hundred years, many foreigners imagine that Magyars wake up to goulash and gulp hot peppers the rest of the day. On the contrary, the use of condiments tends to be subtle, with inspired combinations.

The first Magyars cooked their food in a pot over an open fire. New seasonings and nuances came from France, Italy and Turkey. Paprika was introduced from America in the 17th century, developing over the years into the characteristic piquant, red condiment. The spice is available in "hot" and mild varieties, and although it's the keystone of Hungarian cuisine, many dishes contain no paprika at all. Most food is cooked in lard or rendered fat rather than oil or butter, which sometimes taxes delicate stomachs unaccustomed to the Hungarian method.

Some specialities worth looking for:

Appetizers (*előételek*). For starters try *libamáj-pástétom*, a flaky pastry shell filled with goose-liver paté mixed with butter and béchamel sauce, spices and brandy. *Hortobágyi húsos palacsinta* (pancakes Hortobágy style)—thin pancakes filled with minced meat and dressed with sour cream—make a delicious beginning to a meal. A vegetarian speciality, *paprika-szeletek körözöttel tölive*, combines sliced green peppers, ewe's cheese, spices and beer.

Soup (*levesek*). *Gulyásleves* (goulash soup) is the real thing: chunks of beef, potatoes, onion, tomatoes and peppers, with paprika, caraway seeds and garlic for added flavour. (Note that what is called goulash abroad is a Hungarian meat stew actually named *pörkölt*.) *Szegedi halászlé* (Szeged fisherman's soup) is a sort of paprika-crazed freshwater bouillabaisse: pieces of giant pike-perch and carp boiled in a stock lengthily concocted from fish heads, tails and bones, with onions and, of course, paprika. On a hot summer day, sample *hideg almaleves* (cold apple soup): creamy and refreshing with a dash of cinnamon.

Fish *(halételek)*. *Paprikás ponty* (carp in paprika sauce) and *pisztráng tejszín-mártásban* (trout baked in cream) show the extremes to which the Hungarians go to glamourize their lake and river fish. *Balatoni fogas* (pike-perch from Lake Balaton) is considered a prime delicacy. (Note that some of the fish are equipped with an infinity of tiny bones, slowing the eating.)

Meat *(húsételek)*. *Fatányéros* (mixed grill) combines oversized chunks of pork, beef, veal and perhaps goose liver, roasted over a spit and served on a wooden platter. *Csikós tokány,* called a cowboy dish, consists of strips of beef braised in a mixture of diced bacon, onions, sliced pepper and tomatoes, served with *galuska* (miniature dumplings). Finally, what could be more Hungarian than *töltött paprika* (stuffed pepper)? Green peppers are filled with minced pork, rice, onions, garlic and then blanketed in tomato sauce.

Game and fowl *(vadak, szárnyasok)*. The Hungarian treatment enhances tastes as rich as *vaddisznó* (wild boar) and *őz* (venison). As for poultry, you'll surely be offered *csirke-paprikás* (chicken paprika), with the two main ingredients of the title—plus onion, green peppers, tomato and sour cream.

Sweets *(tészták)*. Do strive to save some strength for the last course, for the Hungarians excel at desserts. The microscopically thin pastry of *rétes* or strudel ought to be framed in the bakers' hall of fame. The adjectives (and fillings) to look for: *almás* (apple), *meggyes* (sour cherry), *mákos* (poppy-seed) and *túrós* (cottage cheese). Or you could go the whole hog with *Gundel palacsinta,* named after a famed Budapest restaurant owner: pancakes filled with a nut-and-raisin paste, drenched in a creamy chocolate and rum sauce and then flambéed. For simpler tastes there are ice-cream *(fagylalt),* cheese *(sajt)* or fruit *(gyümölcs)*.

Hungarian Wines

Most of the wine made in Hungary is white, the most famous and inimitable being Tokay (*Tokaji* on the bottle). The volcanic soil of the Tokaj region, in northeast Hungary, has produced a wine fit for kings since the Middle Ages. It was a favourite of Catherine the Great and Louis XIV, and inspired poetry from Voltaire and song from Schubert. Some prosaic specifications: *Tokaji furmint* is dry; *Tokaji szamorodni,* medium-sweet; and the full-bodied *Tokaji aszú,* very sweet. The quality is graded from 3 to 5 *puttonyos* (points).

Less celebrated but perfectly satisfying white wines come from the Lake Balaton region. Look for the prefixes *Badacsonyi, Bala-*

tonfüredi and *Csopaki*. The Roman emperors liked Balaton wines so much they had them shipped to Rome.

The best known Hungarian red, *Egri bikavér* (Bull's Blood of Eger), is a full-bodied, hearty wine. More subtle is the *pinot noir* from the same district.

Some regional wines to look for in your travels:

Kékfrankos, a deep red wine, comes from the area surrounding Lake Fertő, near Sopron.

Villányi burgundi, from the southernmost vineyards in Hungary, is a prized, smooth red.

The Mecsek region near Pécs accounts for two types of dessert wine, *Rizling* and *Furmint*.

Near the folklore town of Kalocsa, the sandy soil of the Great Plain produces a popular, light red called *Kadarka*.

Waiters are most helpful about wines, so don't hesitate to ask for a recommendation when you order your meal.

Hungarians usually add a splash of soda or mineral water to their table wines, a custom less than a century old. In the Middle Ages, oddly, Hungarians were among the few Europeans who insisted on drinking their wine "straight".

Other Drinks

Hungarian beers go well with heavy, spicy food. Or you have the choice of brews from Czechoslovakia, Austria and perhaps Germany. Well-known international soft drinks are bottled in Hungary, competing with local fizzy products and fruit juices.

Espresso coffee—strong, black, hot and usually sweet—is consumed day and night. There's no alternative except for tea, made to undemanding standards with familiar brands of imported teabags. (The closest you can get to white coffee in most bars is a tiny cup of espresso with a mini-pitcher of milk or cream on the side.)

As an aperitif you may be offered a "puszta cocktail", menacingly blending apricot brandy, digestive bitters and Tokay sweet wine. After dinner, you may want to compare some of Hungary's extraordinarily good fruit brandies *(pálinka)*. Look for *alma* (apple), *barack* (apricot), *cseresznye* (cherry), *körte* (pear) and *szilva* (plum). And now you know what all those beautiful orchards are for.

Tipping

Tipping is very much a fact of life in the People's Republic. If you have been served well, which is most probable, it's customary to tip the waiter 10 to 15 per cent. The waiter who brings the bill and takes your money may not be the one who served you, but don't worry; all the gratuities are pooled.

BERLITZ-INFO

CONTENTS

A ACCOMMODATION

See also CAMPING. It's prudent to book accommodation well in advance, for rooms are often in short supply. The tightest season is the summer, but crowds also descend for trade fairs, exhibitions and major international conferences when you might not expect them. If you arrive without a reservation, though, all is not lost. Tourist information or travel agency offices at the airport, railway stations and border-crossing points can usually arrange for accommodation—in a private home if all else fails.

Hotels *(szálloda)* are graded by the star system: a five-star hotel is truly luxurious, and a one-star budget hotel has few amenities. Most hotels in the three-to-five star class have their own shopping arcades, tourist agency and airline offices. Rates drop by as much as 30% outside the summer tourist season.

Accommodation in **private homes**—a room with or without breakfast, or a self-contained **flat**—can be booked through travel agencies in Budapest and other towns. The rates in Budapest are about the same as those of moderate hotels, but lower in the country.

The equivalent of English "Bed and Breakfast" establishments are found along major roads and in holiday centres. Often the sign *Szoba kiadó* is supplemented by its German equivalent, *Fremdenzimmer*.

Youth accommodation is available in the Summer holiday period only. Contact the Express office at Semmelweiss v. 4; tel.: 176-634.

I'd like a single room/ double room.	**Egyágyas/Kétágyas szobát kérek.**
with bath/with shower	**fürdőszobával/zuhanyozóval**

AIRPORT *(repülőtér)*

All international flights operate from Budapest's Ferihegy Airport, the country's only commercial airfield; there are no domestic flights at all. Among the facilities at Ferihegy: porters, baggage trolleys, currency exchange desks, accommodation and car hire desks, a news-stand, a buffet and restaurant, a post office with international telegraph service and a duty-free shop. Terminal 1 serves foreign airlines, while Terminal 2 is reserved for the use of MALÉV, the Hungarian national airline.

It takes half an hour to travel from the airport to the centre of Budapest. MALÉV operates an airport bus service between Ferihegy (on the south-east outskirts of Budapest) and the Engels tér bus terminal (platform 1):

Ferihegy—Budapest centre, every half hour from 6 a.m. to 10.30 p.m.
Budapest centre—Ferihegy, every half hour from 5 a.m. to 10 p.m.

Where do I get the bus to the city centre/to the airport?	**Hol a buszmegálló a városközpont felé/a repülőtér felé?**

BABY-SITTERS   B

Except for the luxury hotels, which can usually arrange for baby-sitters and provide cots, highchairs, etc., this could be a problem, since no organized sitter service exists in Hungary. It may come to mobilizing one of the hotel maids or a friend of the desk clerk, and there may well be a language problem.

Can you get me/us a baby-sitter for tonight?	**Tudna nekem/nekünk biztosítani ma estére egy baby-sittert?**

CAMPING *(kemping)*   C

More than 200 campsites, big and small, are scattered around Hungary, with the biggest concentration on the shores of Lake Balaton. Budapest itself has two large camping grounds. All the sites in the country are graded according to international standards. The top (three-star) establishments have more facilities, a larger area for each family, and tents and cabins for hire. In general, the camping season lasts from May to September, but a few sites open earlier in the year and continue operating into the wintry weather.

The Hungarian Camping and Caravanning Club issues a detailed map and a list of the major campsites and their facilities—from supermarkets and currency exchange offices to beaches and nightclubs:

Magyar Camping és Caravanning Club—MCCC
Üllői út 6, H-1088 Budapest VIII.; tel. 336-536.

CAR HIRE

See also Driving. Hiring a car in Hungary involves no special problems; arrangements and conditions are similar to those encountered elsewhere. The minimum age requirement is 21, and the driver should be in possession of a valid licence, held for at least one year. A deposit has to be paid, though this is normally waived for holders of accepted cards. Bills must be settled in hard currency. All cars are insured, but supplementary coverage is available at an extra charge.

Although international car hire firms do not operate directly in Hungary, companies like Hertz, Avis, InterRent and others have arrangements with Hungarian state agencies such as IBUSZ Cooptourist and Volántourist. Cars, with or without drivers, may be booked either directly through these agencies or through travel bureaux in hotels, at the airport, etc.

| I'd like to hire a car. | **Egy kocsit szeretnék bérelni.** |
| *large/small* | **nagy/kis** |

CIGARETTES, CIGARS, TOBACCO *(cigaretta, szivar, dohány)*

Shops called *Dohánybolt* or *Trafik* stock tobacco products, as do most hotels and supermarkets. A wide range of cigarettes from Hungary and neighbouring countries are available at relatively low prices. Intertourist shops sell hard-to-get foreign brands for hard currency.

Restrictions on smoking cover most public places, including all cinemas, theatres and concert halls. Smoking is banned on public transport, including the ticket and waiting-room areas of railway stations. But long-distance trains have some smoking carriages.

I'd like a packet of cigarettes.	**Kérek egy csomag cigarettát.**
filter-tipped/without filter	**filteres/filter nélküli**
A box of matches, please.	**Egy doboz gyufát kérek.**

CLIMATE AND CLOTHING

Hungary boasts about its 2,000 hours of sunshine a year, which is justified all in all as it does better than the average for Central Europe. July and August tend to be the most warm and sunny months, when there's the most happening, but temperatures stay mild from early May to the end of October.

Temperate though Hungary may be, temperatures have a habit of jumping about all over the place at short notice: while an average July day may seem ideal at around 20 °C (68 °F), suddenly it might soar to a tropical swelter or sink to a brisk chill with little warning. So summer visitors should pack for all eventualities and raincoats might turn out welcome for some summer nights. In winter, be prepared for snow and bracing cold. Average daily temperatures in Budapest:

	J	F	M	A	M	J	J	A	S	O	N	D
°F	27	34	43	54	63	68	72	72	64	52	43	34
°C	−3	1	6	12	17	20	22	22	18	11	6	1

As for formality, a certain Central European seriousness persists, though there are no definite rules. Evening gowns and dark suits are standard at the Opera House, but jeans are also acceptable. On warm summer days, jackets and ties are abandoned in most areas of life. Headwaiters don't discriminate against informally dressed clients. For official or business meetings, suits are appropriate but by no means essential.

COMMUNICATIONS

Post offices *(postahivatal)*. Local post offices are usually open from 8 a.m. to 5 p.m., Monday to Friday, and until noon or 1 p.m. on Saturdays. Main post offices operate from 7 p.m. until 8 p.m., Monday to Saturday.

Post offices handle mail, telephone, telegraph and telex services, but not international money transfers. Stamps *(bélyeg)* can also be bought at tobacconists or where postcards are sold. Postboxes are painted red and usually decorated with a hunting horn.

The use of poste-restante (general-delivery) service is not widespread in Hungary. It's better to have letters addressed to your hotel or, if your exact plans are uncertain, to your embassy.

Telephone *(telefon)*, **telegrams** *(távirat)* **and telex.** Call boxes (telephone booths) for local calls are usually green-and-yellow or white, while those for international calls are red. Illustrated, self-explanatory instructions are posted. Long-distance and international calls are best made through your hotel switchboard or at a post office.

In Budapest, a modern international telecommunications centre with all telephone, telegraph and telex services operates at the corner of Petőfi Sándor utca and Martinelli tér (Budapest V.) from 7 a.m. to 8 p.m., Monday to Friday, and until 7 p.m. on Saturdays, with limited service on Sunday mornings and public holidays.

Directory enquiries in foreign languages, tel. 172-200 in Budapest.

express (special delivery)	**expressz küldemény**
registered	**ajánlott**
airmail	**légiposta**
I'd like a stamp for this letter/ this postcard, please.	**Kérek egy bélyeget erre a levélre/ a képeslapra.**
I'd like to send a telegram.	**Táviratot szeretnék feladni.**

COMPLAINTS

Every establishment in Hungary has a "complaint book" *(vásárlók könyve)* on the premises, but problems are resolved slowly through such channels. It's much wiser to try to sort out any difficulties face-to-face with the manager. Above all, relax and keep your temper in check. Threats will never work; good humour may well.

CONVERTER CHARTS

Hungary uses the metric system. The only slight variation from standard European practice is that most products in food markets are sold and labelled in dekagrams rather than grams (10 dekagrams = 100 grams = 3½ ounces).

Temperature

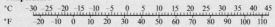

Length

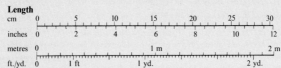

Weight

grams 0   100 200 300 400 500 600 700 800 900 1 kg
ounces 0   4   8   12 1 lb. 20 24 28 2 lb.

Fluid measures

imp.gals. 0   5   10

litres 0   5   10   20   30   40   50

U.S.gals. 0   5   10

Kilometres to miles

km 0 1 2 3 4 5 6   8   10   12   14   16
miles 0 ½ 1 1½ 2   3   4   5   6   7   8   9   10

CRIME AND THEFT

Though violent crime is rare in Hungary, visitors ought to take elementary precautions to protect their property. This means locking car doors and hotel rooms. When you park your car, place valuables out of sight or lock them in the luggage compartment. Don't leave jewellery, money or documents around but use the hotel's safe.

CUSTOMS *(vám)* AND ENTRY REGULATIONS

See also DRIVING. Everyone needs a valid passport to visit Hungary. In addition (except for citizens of Finland, Austria and the socialist countries), everyone needs a visa. This may be obtained through travel agents or direct from any Hungarian diplomatic mission—it usually takes less than 48 hours. If you haven't the time, you can arrive without a visa and be issued one at the frontier or airport (but train passengers must have visas in advance). Visas are generally valid for a maximum 30-day visit, which can be extended.

Green and red customs channels are provided at the airport and at Austrian border crossing points. If you have nothing to declare, use the green lane (spot checks do take place). Here are the main items you may take into Hungary duty-free and, upon your return home, into your own country:

Into:	Cigarettes	Cigars	Tobacco	Spirits	Wine
Hungary	250	or 50	or 250 g.	1 l. and	2 l.
Australia	200	or 250 g.	or 250 g.	1 l. or	1 l.
Canada	200	and 50	and 900 g.	1.1 l. or	1.1 l.
Eire	200	or 50	or 250 g.	1 l. and	2 l.
N. Zealand	200	or 50	or ½ lb.	1 qt. and	1 qt.
S. Africa	400	and 50	and 250 g.	1 l. and	1 l.
U.K.	200	or 50	or 250 g.	1 l. and	2 l.
U.S.A.	200	and 100	and *	1 l. or	1 l.
* A reasonable quantity.					

Among the items forbidden: narcotics, explosives, weapons, and materials deemed obscene or ideologically subversive.

Currency restrictions. Visitors may be required to report the currencies they're carrying, though there is no limit on the foreign funds permitted. As for Hungarian currency, it is forbidden to arrive with or to take out more than 100 forints, and that only in coins. Note that there is a restriction on the amount of forints that may be re-exchanged when leaving the country.

Registration. If you're staying at a hotel, campsite or officially recognized guest accommodation, registration will be done automatically. (You'll have to leave your passport at the hotel desk overnight.) But if you stay in unofficial private accommodation, your host is responsible for having you registered within 48 hours.

Leaving Hungary. The customs officer may ask what you're taking out of the country in the way of commodities and currencies (see also VAT below). Keep handy all sales slips and currency exchange receipts. Aside from museum-worthy antiques and works of art, which require special permits for export, the only customs problem which might surprise you concerns food: you can take out of Hungary only enough food to be used during your travels, for a maximum of three days, including no more than 500 grams of any one kind of food. Salami hoarders beware! For full details on the ins and outs of customs regulations, see the leaflets at travel agencies and hotels. Sales slips for items purchased in hard-currency shops serve as export permits.

VAT. VAT (sales tax) of 25% is included in the purchase price of most goods in Hungary. Foreign tourists buying a minimum 25,000—forint worth of goods in one shop at one time can demand a VAT certificate, have it stamped at the border customs and claim back the VAT amount in hard currency—providing they can prove with exchange receipts that they have changed their hard currency to forint in excess of their purchases.

I have nothing to declare.	**Nincs elvámolni valóm.**

D DRIVING IN HUNGARY

To take your car into Hungary you need: passport and visa; valid driving licence; car registration papers; adequate insurance.

Cars from most European countries are automatically considered to be fully insured, with these exceptions: vehicles from France, Italy, Portugal, Spain, Greece, Turkey and Iceland, which must carry proof of insurance ("green card").

Driving regulations. Cars must be fitted with a nationality plate or sticker and rubber mudguards. You are required to carry a set of spare bulbs, a first-aid kit and a red warning triangle for display in case of an accident or breakdown. The driver and front-seat passenger must use seat belts; children under six are prohibited from travelling in the front seat. Drivers and passengers of motorcycles and scooters have to wear crash helmets. It is not permitted to lend a foreign-registered car to anyone, Hungarian or foreigner.

Drive on the right and pass on the left. Hungary's accident rate is one of Europe's highest. Drive with special vigilance until you've had time to take the measure of the local drivers. At road crossings where signs indicate no priorities, the vehicle on the right has the right of way. Pedestrians have the right of way at pedestrian crossings, marked with white stripes. (If you're a pedestrian, don't count on it!)

In built-up areas, blowing the horn is forbidden except, of course, if it helps prevent an accident. At night and when visibility is poor, headlights should be dipped. On any road except a motorway (expressway), be alert for unexpected obstacles—livestock, horse-drawn wagons and bicycles, for instance. These can pose a real danger. There are more than 9,000 railway level crossings in Hungary, most of them unprotected by gates or barriers but all clearly marked. Approach them with caution.

Hungary's expanding motorway system is well maintained. Yellow emergency telephones are spaced every 2 kilometres (1¼ miles) along the Budapest–Balaton expressway.

Speed limits. Limits are 120 kilometres per hour (75 mph) on four-lane motorways, 100 kph (60 mph) on two-lane motorways, 80 kph (50 mph) on other roads and 60 kph (37 mph) in built-up areas (signalled by a white rectangular sign announcing the name of a town or village). Limits are lower for buses, heavy lorries, cars towing caravans (trailers) and motorcycles.

The police are strict about speeding. You could be fined 1,000 forints on the spot for exceeding the limit, with considerably higher penalties for what's considered dangerous speeding.

Alcohol. In Hungary, drinking and driving are totally, dangerously incompatible. The permissible limit for blood alcohol content is zero; even a glass of beer rings the bell. The law is especially severe on anyone causing an accident while under the influence of alcohol, and on hit-and-run drivers. Foreigners receive no leniency in these cases.

Fuel and oil *(benzin; olaj).* Filling stations are distributed along the motorways and main roads at intervals of 10 to 30 kilometres. On minor roads, they are up to 50 kilometres apart. Stations are usually open from 6 a.m. to 10 p.m. All-night service is available at all Shell and at some major ÁFOR stations. Fuel generally comes in three octane ratings—98, 92, 86—and unleaded (available at about 50 stations country wide).

Fluid measures. See under CONVERTER CHARTS.

Parking. Much of central Budapest has been closed to traffic except for vehicles displaying a special permit. If you leave your car in a prohibited zone, it will be towed away by the police, without exception and without delay. Elsewhere in urban areas, there are automatic parking-ticket vending-machines, or you may be approached by parking attendants who collect a fee and issue official receipts.

Road signs and signposts. Standard international pictographs relate information and warnings on all Hungarian roads. But some information is conveyed in Hungarian: look out in particular for *Útépítés* (Road Works), *Kerülőút* (Diversion Ahead) and *Kőomlás* (Falling Rocks).

Motorways are indicated by green signs, all other main roads by dark blue.

Distances. Here are some approximate road distances in kilometres between Budapest and some regional centres and border-crossing points of interest to users of this guide:

Balatonfüred 130	Pécs 200
Debrecen 225	Rábafüzes 250
Eger 130	Sopron 210
Esztergom 60	Szeged 170
Hegyeshalom 170	Szombathely 220

To convert kilometres to miles, see under CONVERTER CHARTS.

Breakdowns/Accidents. Remember to put out the red warning triangle 50 yards behind your car. Accidents must be reported—to the police in case of personal injury. The "yellow angels" of the Hungarian Automobile Club *(Magyar Autóklub)* come to the rescue of any driver in distress on any major road. They do on-the-spot repairs—free for members of affiliated auto clubs. But finding spare parts for Western-made cars can be a problem of availability as well as of price. The Automobile Club also offers a wide range of services—information, insurance, reservations, guided tours, legal advice. The Club's headquarters is at:

Budapest II., Rómer Flóris u. 4/a; tel. 152-040
For breakdown service in Budapest, telephone 260-668

Full tank, please.	**Kérem, töltse tele a tankot.**
Check the oil/the tires/ the battery, please.	**Ellenőrizze az olajat/a gumikat/az akkumulátort.**
I've had a breakdown.	**Meghibásodott a kocsim.**
There's been an accident.	**Baleset történt.**
Can I park here?	**Szabad itt parkolnom?**

E **ELECTRIC CURRENT**
Throughout Hungary the current is 220-volt, 50-cycle A.C. Plugs are the standard continental type, for which British and North American appliances need an adaptor.

EMBASSIES AND CONSULATES *(nagykövetség; konzulátus)*

Canada	Budapest II., Budakeszi út 32: tel. 767-686/7/8/9
Great Britain	Budapest V., Harmincad u. 6; tel. 182-888
U.S.A.	Budapest V., Szabadság tér 12; tel. 124-224

EMERGENCIES
See also EMBASSIES AND CONSULATES, HEALTH AND MEDICAL CARE, POLICE, etc.

Emergency telephone numbers throughout Hungary:

Ambulance 04
Fire 05
Police 07

GETTING THERE   **G**

Although the types of fares and conditions described below have all been carefully checked, it is advisable to consult a travel agent for the latest information.

From North America

By air

Daily connecting services link the larger American cities to Budapest, primarily via Amsterdam, Copenhagen, Paris, Madrid and Vienna. Toronto, Montreal and Halifax in Canada provide connecting flights every day of the week. Many other Canadian and American cities offer connections on specified days.

There are currently two bargain fares to Budapest. The APEX fare is valid for 14 to 90 days. Reservations and ticketing must be completed 30 days prior to departure and the fare carries a cancellation penalty. Stopovers are not permitted. The 14-to-60-day excursion fare need not be reserved in advance and unlimited stopovers are allowed for a small additional charge. Both APEX and excursion fares are reduced in the low season, from September 15 through to May 14. Children through the age of 11 and youths from 12 to 21 fly for a significant discount.

Charter Flights and Package Tours. Package tours to Bucharest or Transylvania, or to Warsaw, Vienna and Prague, make stops in Budapest. These combined tours last for two weeks and include round-trip air fares and hotels, plus meals and services as specified in each itinerary.

From Great Britain

By air

Scheduled flights depart daily from London to Budapest. You can fly direct, or via Rome or Frankfurt, but there may be an extra charge for flights routed through Vienna.

There are several different fares: first class, excursion, Eurobudget and APEX (Advance Purchase Excursion). APEX fares must be booked at least one month ahead of time. You may stay in the country for between seven and 90 days. Reservations cannot be changed and there are no stopovers. The Eurobudget fare offers more flexibility since there is no minimum or maximum stay, but stopovers are not allowed. Both Eurobudget and APEX fares carry a cancellation fee. The excursion fare can be cancelled without penalty.

Package Tours. Several companies operate packages to Budapest. These holidays usually last for seven nights and include bed, breakfast and the cost of a visa, perhaps even a half-day sightseeing tour. Weekend trips are also available.

By rail

Trains leave from Victoria every morning, arriving at Budapest the following afternoon. The most direct route is via Dover to Ostend and Vienna. Otherwise you can change stations in Paris and continue on the exotic Orient Express by way of Strasbourg, Stuttgart, Munich, Salzburg and Vienna. Bookings should be made several months in advance for this popular train, and even on the Ostend route you must reserve your seat.

An Inter-rail card available to travellers under 26 and valid for a month of unlimited travel in most European countries costs little more than the fare to Budapest. The Rail Europ Senior Card (obtainable before departure only) entitles senior citizens to purchase train tickets for European destinations at a discount.

By hydrofoil

From May through to the end of September a hydrofoil service operates daily on the River Danube from Vienna. Travel time to Budapest averages about 4½ to 5 hours.

By road

Assuming you approach Hungary via Vienna (which is perhaps the most practical way to get there by road), the quickest route is via Ostend through Brussels, Cologne, Nuremberg and Linz, although there are more attractive routes through the countryside. The ferry crossings to Ostend leave from Dover and Folkestone. You can also put your car on a train from Brussels to Salzburg, from which it's a three-hour drive on the motorway to Vienna. From there it's a further 70-odd kilometres to the nearest crossing point at Nickelsdorf/Hegyeshalom. Other border crossing points from Austria are: Klingenbach/Sopron, Rattersdorf/Kőszeg, Heiligenkreuz/Rábafüzes, Schachendorf/Bucsu. From Yugoslavia there are eight crossing points, from Czechoslovakia, seven, from Romania, three and from the USSR, one.

Seven of Hungary's main arteries start from Budapest, with one other from Székesfehérvár, and all of them link up with the European road network.

See also DRIVING IN HUNGARY.

GUIDES AND INTERPRETERS *(idegenvezető; tolmács)*
Guides/interpreters can be hired by the day or half-day through travel agencies in Budapest. These guides, however, may not be qualified to handle the more difficult linguistic problems that arise in certain business or technical discussions. State organizations dealing with foreigners provide staff interpreters for such occasions.

We'd like an English-/French-/ German-speaking guide.	**Egy angolul/franciául/németül beszélő idegenvezetőt kérünk.**

HAIRDRESSERS AND BARBERS *(fodrász; borbély)*   **H**
Even in small neighbourhood shops the service is expert and accommodating... and very cheap by Western standards. "Firstclass" establishments in the luxury hotels charge only slightly higher prices. Tipping is customary; give about 15%.

haircut	**hajvágás**
shampoo and set	**mosás és berakás**
shampoo and blow-dry	**mosás és szárítás**
permanent wave	**tartós hullám**
colour rinse	**festés**
Not too short.	**Ne nagyon rövidre.**
A little more off (here).	**(Itt) Egy kicsit többet kérek levágni.**

HEALTH AND MEDICAL CARE
Many visitors come to Hungary from abroad to regain their health at the therapeutic baths which make this one of Europe's leading spa countries. And if an accident or sudden illness should interfere with

173

your holiday, the Hungarian National Health Service (abbreviated *Sz.T.K.*) and the emergency squad *(Mentők)* are well equipped to handle any unexpected problems. Most Hungarian doctors and dentists also have private practices. To find one, ask at your hotel desk or at your consulate for local doctors speaking English.

The tap water *(csapvíz)* is safe to drink anywhere in Hungary unless it's otherwise announced: *Nem ivóvíz.*

Pharmacies. Look for the sign *gyógyszertár* or *patika.* In Hungary these shops sell only pharmaceutical and related products—not the wide assortment of goods available in their British or American counterparts. (For toiletries and cosmetics, go to an *illatszerbolt;* for photo supplies, to a *fotószaküzlet.*)

Several Budapest pharmacies stay open round the clock. Their addresses are always displayed on an illuminated sign in the window of every other pharmacy.

Where's the nearest pharmacy?	Hol a legközelebbi patika?
I need a doctor/dentist.	Orvosra/Fogorvosra van szükségem.
I have a pain here.	Itt érzek fájdalmat.
headache	fejfájás
stomach ache	gyomorfájás
a fever/a cold	láz/megfázás

HITCH-HIKING *(autóstop)*
Public transport in Hungary is good and cheap so there's not much cause for hitch-hiking. It is not illegal, but not encouraged, either.

HOURS
See also COMMUNICATIONS and MONEY MATTERS. Most shops are open from 10 a.m. (some food shops from 6 or 7 a.m.) to 6 p.m., Monday to Friday, and some until 2 p.m. on Saturdays. Only a few establishments—mostly tobacconists, florists and pastry shops—stay open on Sundays. Department stores operate from 9 a.m. to 7 p.m., Monday to Friday, and until 2 p.m. on Saturdays. Department stores and many shops are open until 7 p.m. on Thursdays.

Hairdressers work from as early as 6 or 7 a.m. to as late as 9 p.m., Monday to Friday, until 4 p.m. on Saturdays.

Museums generally are open from 10 a.m. to 6 p.m., daily except Mondays and certain holidays (admission free on Saturdays). Some small museums operate fewer hours, so check before you go.

LANGUAGE

Hungarian, which is totally unrelated to the languages of surrounding countries, is the mother tongue of more than 95% of the population. The people speak very clearly, without slurs or swallowed sounds; since every word is stressed on the first syllable, a sort of monotone often ensues.

By far the most widely known foreign language is German. A minority of Hungarians (mostly the younger generation) know English, and even fewer know some French. All Hungarians study Russian for four years in secondary school.

The Berlitz phrase book HUNGARIAN FOR TRAVELLERS covers most of the situations you are likely to encounter in Hungary.

LAUNDRY AND DRY-CLEANING *(mosoda; vegytisztító)*

Hotels usually take care of laundry and cleaning problems with dispatch. If you're staying elsewhere, look for the sign *Patyolat*, which indicates an establishment handling both laundry and dry-cleaning. The larger shops may offer express service.

LOST PROPERTY

In Budapest, a central bureau, Talált Tárgyak Központi Hivatala, deals with lost-and-found problems:
Budapest V., Engels tér 5; tel. 174-961

A separate office handles property found on vehicles of the Budapest public-transport system:
Budapest VII., Akácfa utca 18; tel. 226-613

I've lost my wallet/my handbag/ my passport.	**Elvesztettem az irattárcámat/ a kézitáskámat/az útlevelemet.**

MAPS

Travel bureaux give out free maps of Hungary. In each city and town, very detailed maps of the local scene are sold at news-stands, bookstores and travel agencies. The maps in this book were prepared by Cartographia of Budapest which, among many other publications, issues the definitive road atlas of Hungary *(Magyarország Autóatlasza)*, including sketches of virtually every town in the country.

I'd like a street map.	**Egy várostérképet kérnék.**
I'd like a road map of this region.	**Egy erre a vidékre vonatkozó térképet kérnék.**

MEETING PEOPLE

Hungarians are open and friendly. They are so helpful to foreigners that, if you unfold a map on the street, they may give you directions whether you're lost or not. Because their language is so outlandish, they are genuinely delighted when a foreigner attempts to say a few words in Hungarian.

MONEY MATTERS

Currency. The Hungarian *forint* (abbreviated *Ft.*) is divided into 100 *fillér (f)*.
Coins: 10, 20 and 50 f and Ft. 1, 2, 5, 10 and 20.
Banknotes: Ft. 10, 20, 50, 100, 500 and 1,000.

For details of restrictions on import of Hungarian currency, see CUSTOMS AND ENTRY REGULATIONS.

Banks and currency exchange. Official foreign-exchange facilities are found in most banks, hotels and motels, at larger campsites, at travel agencies and in some department stores, as well as at most border crossing points. Or you can go to a branch of the Hungarian National Bank *(Magyar Nemzeti Bank)*, the National Savings Bank *(Országos Takarékpénztár–OTP)* or the Hungarian Foreign Trade Bank *(Magyar Külkereskedelmi Bank)*.

Banking hours are generally from 9 a.m. to 5 p.m., Monday to Friday, and 9 a.m. to 2 p.m. on Saturdays.

Remember to take your passport with you, and be sure to keep all receipts. To reconvert forints into foreign currency when you leave Hungary, you must show the relevant receipt. For VAT regulations, see p. 168.

It is illegal to sell foreign currency to private citizens; don't be tempted by offers in the street—you risk being arrested.

Credit cards and traveller's cheques. Many tourist-oriented establishments—hotels, restaurants, shops, travel agencies—are geared to accept international credit cards; you'll see the signs on the door. Traveller's cheques and Eurocheques are also easy to cash. Some shops, such as Intertourist branches, deal *only* in foreign currency transactions, accepting cash, traveller's cheques and credit cards.

I want to change some pounds/dollars.	**Fontot/Dollárt szeretnék beváltani.**
Do you accept traveller's cheques?	**Traveller's csekket elfogadnak?**
Can I pay with this credit card?	**Ezzel a hitelkártyával fizethetek?**

NEWSPAPERS AND MAGAZINES *(újság; folyóirat)*

The Hungarian news agency MTI publishes a daily (except Sunday and Monday) bilingual English-German paper, *Daily News/Neueste Nachrichten*, displayed at most hotels and on almost every newsstand in Budapest. Widely available, as well, are the newspapers of foreign communist parties.

Kiosks in the capital also sell a selection of Western newspapers and magazines, including the *Times* of London, the *International Herald Tribune* (edited in Paris), and the weeklies *Time* and *Newsweek*. Dailies from the West arrive with one day's delay.

A free monthly magazine, *Programme in Hungary*, has parallel texts in German, English and French.

The journal *New Hungarian Quarterly*, published in English, offers profound insights into Hungarian life, culture and politics.

Have you any English-language newspapers?	**Van angolnyelvű újságjuk?**

PHOTOGRAPHY P

Hungarian shops sell international brands of film but by no means always what you need in size or type. To be sure you don't run out of your preferred brand, it's wise to carry an adequate supply from home. Film can be processed in Budapest but not very rapidly, so it's usually better to take your exposed film home for development.

The Hungarians are easy about being photographed, but use sense concerning what, who, when and where. All military installations and other sensitive places are advertised by "no photography" warning signs.

Some airport security machines use X-rays which can ruin your film. Ask that it be checked separately, or enclose it in a lead-lined bag.

I'd like some film for this camera.	**Ehhez a géphez kérnék filmet.**
black-and-white film	**fekete fehér film**
colour prints	**színes kópiák**
colour slides	**színes diák**
35-mm	**harmincöt milliméter**
super-8	**szuper nyolcas**
How long will it take to develop this film?	**Meddig tart előhívni ezt a filmet?**
May I take a picture?	**Lefényképezhetem?**

POLICE *(rendőrség)*

See also EMERGENCIES. Police wear blue-and-grey uniforms. Traffic police and highway patrols dress similarly but with white caps and white leather accessories to make them more visible. Police cars are blue and white. There is no special police unit detailed to deal with tourist enquiries but the police in general are helpful to foreigners.

Where is the nearest police station?	**Hol a legközelebbi rendőrség?**

PRICES

To give you an idea of what to expect, here are some average prices in Hungarian forints (Ft.), except in those cases where prices are normally quoted in U.S. dollars. However, due to inflation as well as seasonal and regional variations these figures must be regarded as approximate, and we cannot vouch for their accuracy.

Airport transfer. Taxi to central Budapest Ft. 230–280, airline bus Ft. 20.

Camping. Daily rate per person with car and tent or caravan (trailer) Ft. 150–400.

Car hire. $25–80 per day plus $0.25–0.80 per kilometre.

Cigarettes (per packet of 20). Hungarian Ft. 16–40, Western (made in Hungary under licence) Ft. 32–40, Western imported Ft. 70–100.

Entertainment. Theatre Ft. 200 and up, opera Ft. 300 and up, discotheque Ft. 100, nightclub (minimum) Ft. 300 per person.

Excursions. Half-day Ft. 500, full-day to Ft. 1,000.

Hairdresser. *Woman's* haircut Ft. 300, shampoo and set or blow-dry Ft. 700, permanent wave from Ft. 800. *Man's* haircut Ft. 100.

Hotels (double room with bath and breakfast). ***** $150, *** $80–90, * $25–30.

Meals and drinks. Lunch in moderate restaurant approx. Ft. 300, in expensive restaurant Ft. 1,000. Dinner *à la carte,* moderate Ft. 1,600, expensive Ft. 2,500. Bottle of wine, expensive Ft. 300, beer Ft. 100, soft drink Ft. 60–80.

Supermarket. Bread Ft. 14 per kilo, litre of milk Ft. 12–15, butter Ft. 30 for 250 grams, cheese Ft. 120 per kilo, instant coffee (imported) Ft. 200 for 50 grams, salami Ft. 400 per kilo, eggs Ft. 50 per dozen.

Transport. Budapest city bus Ft. 3, tram Ft. 2, metro Ft. 2. Sample taxi fares: Castle District to Heroes' Square (Hősök tere) Ft. 70, Vigadó tér to Opera Ft. 40–45.

PUBLIC HOLIDAYS *(hivatalos ünnep)*

January 1	Újév	New Year's Day
April 4	A felszabadulás ünnepe	Liberation Day
May 1	A munka ünnepe	Labour Day
August 20	Az alkotmány napja	Constitution Day
November 7	A forradalom ünnepe	Revolution Day
December 25	Karácsony első napja	Christmas Day
December 26	Karácsony második napja	Boxing Day
Movable date:	*Húsvét hétfő*	Easter Monday

Are you open tomorrow? **Holnap nyitva tartanak?**

RADIO AND TV

Very brief news bulletins for foreigners are broadcast, in summer only, on Budapest Radio and on TV.

Hungarian television broadcasts in colour on two channels, daily except most Mondays. On Channel 2 some imported programmes are transmitted in the original language. The better hotels offer western cable TV in English, as well as in-house video programmes. Both radio and television carry bundles of commercials from time to time.

To catch up with the news, you'll need a transistor radio powerful enough to pick up European stations on medium wave at night, or the short-wave transmissions of Voice of America, the BBC, Radio Canada International, etc.

RELIGIOUS SERVICES *(istentisztelet)*

The great majority of Hungarians are Roman Catholics. Other religions are also represented, most notably Protestant, Eastern Orthodox and Jewish. While most churches are open to the public, there are no services expressly for foreigners. If you visit a historic church for sightseeing purposes while a service is in progress, stay in the rear of the building so as not to disturb the worshippers.

RESTAURANTS

Hungary's 18,000 or so eating places are divided into a dozen or more categories, none of them, unfortunately, called a "restaurant". If you see the sign "restaurant", it normally means foreign tourists are catered for. Other, more frequently encountered terminology:

Bisztró: small and reasonably priced restaurant.

Büfé: serves hot and cold snacks.

179

Csárda: country inn, often with regional atmosphere and music.
Étterem: restaurant serving a wide range of food and drinks, with prices pegged to its classification—luxury, first, second or third class.
Önkiszolgáló: inexpensive self-service snack bar.
Snackbar: an *önkiszolgáló* with pretensions.
Vendéglő: restaurant service with moderate prices and rustic decor.

Many eating places have been franchised to private operators. The profit motive has upgraded them while the competition encourages the standard state-run establishments to do better.

By law, all eating places must offer at least two set menus *(napi menü)* every day. These low-priced "package deals" usually include soup, a main course and dessert.

The *à la carte* menu is long and complicated. Even if you find a menu translated into a language you understand, a certain amount of confusion is inevitable. Desserts, for instance, are normally printed on the first, not the last page. Drinks often appear on a separate list and may be served by a different waiter.

When to eat

Breakfast *(reggeli)* is served between 7 and 10 a.m. Some establishments provide a "continental" version—bread and rolls, butter and jam, coffee or tea. However, many provincial hotels routinely add eggs, cold meats, cheese and yoghurt.

Lunch *(ebéd)* is eaten between noon and 2 or 3 p.m. It's the main meal of the day for most people. This means soup, a main course and dessert, with beer or wine or soft drinks, followed by coffee.

At dinner *(vacsora)*, from 7 to 10 or 11 p.m., people usually skip the soup and may forego the meat course for a cold plate. Wine is the most popular accompaniment.

Asking the waiter

Could we have a table?	**Lenne szabad asztaluk?**		
The bill, please.	**Kérem a számlát.**		
Keep the change.	**A többi a magáé.**		
I'd like...	**Kérnék...**		
beer	**sört**	fruit juice	**gyümölcslét**
bread	**kenyeret**	lemonade	**limonádét**
butter	**vajat**	meat	**húst**
cheese	**sajtot**	milk	**tejet**
coffee	**kávét**	mineral water	**ásványvizet**
fish	**halat**	mustard	**mustárt**

noodles	metéltet
potatoes	burgonyát
rice	rizst
salad	salátát
salt	sót
sandwich	szendvicset

soup	levest
sugar	cukrot
tea	teát
vegetables	főzeléket
water	vizet
wine	bort

Reading the menu

alma	*apple*	hagyma	*onions*
aranygaluska	*sweet dumpling*	halsaláta	*fish salad*
ananas	*pineapple*	húsleves	*meat soup*
bableves	*bean soup*	italok	*drinks*
bakonyi	*"outlaw" soup*	kacsa	*duck*
betyárleves		káposzta	*cabbage*
bárányhús	*lamb*	kappan	*capon*
békacomb	*frog's legs*	kapucineres	*coffee soufflé*
borda	*chop*	felfújt	
borjúhús	*veal*	kolbászfélék	*sausages*
burgonya	*potatoes*	liba	*goose*
citrom	*lemon*	málna	*raspberries*
cseresznye	*cherries*	marhahús	*beef*
csirke	*chicken*	meggy	*sour cherries*
csuka	*pike*	narancs	*orange*
dinsztelve	*braised*	nyelvhal	*sole*
dió	*nuts*	nyúl	*rabbit*
diszóhús	*pork*	őszibarack	*peach*
édeskömény	*caraway seeds*	palacsinta	*pancakes*
eper	*strawberries*	paradiscom	*tomatoes*
erőleves	*consommé*	ponty	*carp*
húsgombóccal	*with meat dumplings*	pörkölt	*stew*
		pulyka	*turkey*
fasirozott	*meatballs*	ráksaláta	*crab salad*
fogas	*pike-perch*	ribizli	*red currants*
fokhagyma	*garlic*	rántva	*breaded*
főve	*broiled*	rostélyos	*stewed steak*
galuska	*dumplings*	saláta	*lettuce*
gesztenye	*chestnuts*	sárgabarack	*apricot*
gomba	*mushrooms*	sárgarépa	*carrots*
görögdinnye	*watermelon*	sonka	*ham*
gulyásleves	*goulash (soup)*	sülve	*roasted*

sültkrumpli	*French fries*	**vegyesfőzelék**	*mixed*	
sütve	*fried*		*vegetables*	
töltött	*stuffed*	**zeller**	*celery*	
uborka	*cucumber*	**zöldborsó**	*peas*	

T TIME DIFFERENCES

Hungary follows Central European Time, GMT + 1. In summer, the clock is put one hour ahead (GMT + 2). Summer chart:

New York	London	**Budapest**	Jo'burg	Sydney	Auckland
6 a.m.	11 a.m.	**noon**	noon	8 p.m.	10 p.m.

What time is it, please? **Hány óra?**

TIPPING

Have no fear of giving offence if you offer a tip: the old custom survives in Hungary, and gratuities are expected by a wide assortment of service personnel, as well as taxi drivers and gypsy violinists. There are no iron-clad formulae for the appropriate amount to give, but waiters and taxi drivers normally get 10%, barbers and women's hairdressers 15%. Here are some further suggestions to save the embarrassment of under- or over-tipping.

Porter, per bag	Ft. 30
Bellboy, errand	Ft. 30
Maid, per week	Ft. 200
Doorman, hails cab	Ft. 20
Hat-check	Ft. 20
Lavatory attendant	Ft. 5
Gypsy violinist, for personal attention	Ft. 100–200
Tourist guide (half-day)	Ft. 300
Theatre usher	add Ft. 20 to programme for sale
Filling station attendant	round up amount on pump (+ Ft. 20 for checking air and oil, Ft. 10 for cleaning windscreen)

Keep the change. **A többi a magáé.**

TOILETS

Public conveniences are found in all Hungarian cities—in train or metro stations, parks and squares, museums and, of course, in hotels, restaurants and cafés. The sign may point to *mosdó* or *W.C.* (pronounced *vay*-tsay), and if pictures don't indicate which room is which, you'll have to remember that *férfi* means "men" and *női* means "women".

Where are the toilets?	**Hol a W.C.?**

TOURIST INFORMATION OFFICES *(turista információs iroda)*

The Hungarian travel company IBUSZ has offices in some 15 foreign cities, providing information, tour bookings, etc. Among them:

Great Britain
Danube Travel Ltd., General Agent IBUSZ-Hungary,
6, Conduit Street, London W1R 9TG;
tel. (01) 493-0263

U.S.A.
IBUSZ Hungarian Travel Ltd., 400 Kalby Street, Suite 1104,
Fort Lee, NJ 07024

In Budapest and in all tourist areas, IBUSZ and competing travel agencies such as Budapest Tourist, Cooptourist, Siótour and Volántourist, as well as all regional travel agencies, run networks of offices handling money exchange, housing problems, excursions and general information. They are found in and near hotels, railway stations, busy shopping areas and at the airport. Many are open during normal office hours, but in summer the more important units stay open until 8 or even 10 p.m.

Tourinform. For information by telephone—in English, French, German, Russian or Hungarian—call 426-176 in Budapest, even from abroad. The range of information readily available includes weather forecasts, bus and railway schedules, currency rates, plus events of the day.

The Tourinform service operates from 7 a.m. to 9 p.m., Monday to Friday, to 8 p.m. on Saturdays and from 8 a.m. to 1 p.m. on Sundays at 74–76 Rákoczi-ut.

Where's there a tourist office?	**Hol találok turista irodát?**

TRANSPORT

All Hungarian cities are well provided with efficient and stunningly cheap public transport services. The most comprehensive of all serves Budapest, where no place is more than 500 metres from a bus, tram, trolley bus or metro stop. Maps of all the lines, both surface and underground, are sold at major stations. Transport maps are also available in other major cities (though only Budapest has an underground railway). Day tickets for unlimited travel can be used interchangeably on all forms of public transport.

Budapest's transport system comprises the following:

Buses *(busz)*. Blue Ikarus buses, made in Hungary, cover some 450 miles on more than 200 routes in Budapest. A bus stop is marked by a blue-bordered rectangular sign with the silhouette of a bus and the letter "M"—for *megálló*. At most stops a sketch map of the route, a list of the stops, the hours of operation and even the minimum and maximum number of minutes between buses are posted. You must have a blue ticket *before* you board a bus. Automatic dispensers sell them at major bus stops and pedestrian subways, or you can buy them at metro change booths, travel bureaux and tobacco shops. Inside the bus, validate your ticket in one of the red punching devices near the doors; keep the serial number facing up. Then hold onto your ticket in case an inspector should ask for it. Though you'll see very few passengers punching tickets, it doesn't mean they're dishonest; the majority buy cheap monthly passes allowing unlimited travel. Signal at the door when you want to get off.

Trolley buses *(trolibusz)*. To save fuel, these lines are being expanded. But they still constitute only a tiny proportion of the whole municipal system. Use a yellow tram ticket.

Trams *(villamos)*. Yellow trams or streetcars, usually in trains of three or four, cover a 120-mile network. Ten of the 50 tram lines run all night. You need a yellow tram ticket which you must validate on board. The same tickets also serve on the suburban railway within the city limits, and the original Millenary underground (subway) line, now called metro No. 1.

Underground *(földalatti* or *metró)*. Underground (subway) line No. 1, the Millenary line, was opened in 1896—the first in continental Europe. It operates modern tram-like cars and requires a yellow tram ticket. The new metro lines, 2 and 3, use Soviet wide-gauge trains. Some of the stations are quite spacious and splendid. All three lines converge at Deák tér, but there is no free transfer.

Trains *(vonat)*. Budapest has three suburban commuter lines *(HÉV)*, of which the Batthyány tér to Szentendre route is of interest to tourists. When you want to get off one of these trains you have to slide the door open by hand. It closes again automatically.

Inter-city trains run by Hungarian State Railways *(Magyar Államvasutak—MÁV)* operate from three Budapest stations—the historic Keleti (East) and Nyugati (West) stations and the spacious modern Déli (South) terminal. First- and second-class tickets are sold, as well as rail passes good for seven or ten days of unlimited travel within Hungary. (Train compartments are marked 1 and 2.)

Taxis. Metered vehicles both state-owned and private serve Budapest, mostly from taxi ranks near the big hotels, metro and train stations. They can also be hailed on the street when the roof sign saying "Taxi" is lit. Taxis can also be summoned by phone: 222-222 or 666-666. Private taxis are usually cleaner and the drivers, more polite.

Boats. Motor launches ply the Budapest section of the Danube from about 9 a.m. to 8 p.m. daily during the tourist season. Bus tickets are used. Among the principal stations are Gellért tér, Batthyány tér and Petőfi tér, and there are several stops on Margaret Island. Sightseeing excursion boats operate from Vigadó tér, from where boats and hydrofoils leave for Visegrád and Esztergom.

I want a ticket to ...	Kérek egy jegyet ...-ba/-be/-ra/ -re*.
single (one-way)	egy útra
return (round-trip)	oda-vissza
first/second class	első/másod osztály
Will you tell me when to get off?	Megmondaná, hol szálljak ki?

---

* In Hungarian, prepositions are replaced by suffixes. Choose one that sounds harmonious with the place name.

USEFUL EXPRESSIONS

yes/no	**igen/nem**
please/thank you	**kérem/köszönöm**
excuse me/you're welcome	**bocsásson meg/szívesen**
sorry	**sajnálom**
where/when/how	**hol/mikor/hogy**
yesterday/today/tomorrow	**tegnap/ma/holnap**
day/week/month/year	**nap/hét/hónap/év**
north/south	**észak/dél**
east/west	**kelet/nyugat**
good/bad	**jó/rossz**
big/small	**nagy/kicsi**
cheap/expensive	**olcsó/drága**
old/new	**régi/új**
here/there	**itt/ott**
near/far	**közel/távol**
left/right	**bal/jobb**
first/last	**első/utolsó**
early/late	**korán/későn**
Good morning.	**Jó reggelt.**
Good afternoon.	**Jó napot.**
Good evening.	**Jó estét.**
Good night.	**Jó éjszakát.**
Goodbye.	**Viszontlátásra.**
Do you speak English/French/ German?	**Beszél angolul/franciául/ németül?**
What does this mean?	**Ez mit jelent?**
Slowly, please.	**Lassan, kérem.**
I don't understand.	**Nem értem.**
Do you understand?	**Ön érti?**
Could you repeat it?	**Megismételné?**
Please write it down.	**Kérem, írja ezt le.**
Waiter!/Waitress!	**Pincér!/Pincérnő!**
Taxi, please.	**Taxi, kérem.**
I'd like...	**Kérnék ...**
How much is it?	**Mibe kerül?**
Thank you, this is for you.	**Köszönöm. Ez a magáé.**
Just a minute.	**Egy pillanat.**
Help me please.	**Segítene kérem.**
Can you direct me to...?	**Elvezetne a...?**
What time is it?	**Hány óra?**

NUMBERS

0	nulla	13	tizenhárom	40	negyven
1	egy	14	tizennégy	50	ötven
2	kettő	15	tizenöt	60	hatvan
3	három	16	tizenhat	70	hetven
4	négy	17	tizenhét	80	nyolcvan
5	öt	18	tizennyolc	90	kilencven
6	hat	19	tizenkilenc	100	egyszáz
7	hét	20	húsz	101	százegy
8	nyolc	21	huszonegy	200	kettőszáz
9	kilenc	22	huszonkettő	300	háromszáz
10	tíz	23	huszonhárom	500	ötszáz
11	tizenegy	30	harminc	1,000	egyezer
12	tizenkettő	31	harmincegy	2,000	kétezer

DAYS OF THE WEEK

Monday	**hétfő**	*Friday*	**péntek**
Tuesday	**kedd**	*Saturday*	**szombat**
Wednesday	**szerda**	*Sunday*	**vasárnap**
Thursday	**csütörtök**		

MONTHS

January	**január**	*July*	**július**
February	**február**	*August*	**augusztus**
March	**március**	*September*	**szeptember**
April	**április**	*October*	**október**
May	**május**	*November*	**november**
June	**június**	*December*	**december**

SIGNS AND NOTICES

Bejárat	*Entrance*	**Meleg**	*Hot*
Dohányzó	*Smoking permitted*	**Műemlék**	*Monument*
		Nyitva	*Open*
Fel	*Up*	**Szabad**	*Vacant*
Felvilágosítás	*Information*	**Tilos**	*No smoking*
Foglalt	*Occupied*	**a dohányzás**	
Hideg	*Cold*	**Tólni**	*Push*
Húzni	*Pull*	**Veszély**	*Danger*
Kijárat	*Exit*	**Vigyázat**	*Caution*
Le	*Down*	**Zárva**	*Closed*

INDEX

An asterisk (*) next to a page number indicates a map reference. Where there's more than one number, the one in bold type refers to the main entry. To facilitate quick finding, we have separated the complete Budapest index from that to the rest of the country. For index to Practical Information, see p. 160.

Budapest

The figure in brackets following the map page number refers to the site on the map (pp. 10, 11, 12, 13) and corresponds to the number in the key on p. 14.

General Index

048/904 SUD 26